THE GREAT
NEW ZEALAND
BAKING
BOOK

THE GREAT
NEW ZEALAND
BAKING
BOOK

ALLYSON GOFTON

Photography by Alan Gillard

David Bateman

Dedication

To my Mum —
Mother is another word for Love

Special thanks

Allyson wishes to thank Murray
Wham and Richard Devine and
Defiance Flour Mills Ltd. (Elfin),
Elizabeth Stewart, Michael Robertson
and Chelsea Sugar, for supplying
flours, cooking brans, baking powders,
custard powders, and sugars for the
testing of this book.

With Elfin, everything turns out for the best.

First published in 1994 by David Bateman Ltd.,
30 Tarndale Grove, Albany, Auckland, New Zealand.

ISBN 1 86953 165 5

Typeset by Bryan Coppersmith, Auckland
Printed in Hong Kong through Colorcraft Ltd.
Design by Errol McLeary
Photographs by Alan Gillard

Contents

INTRODUCTION

My childhood is full of wonderful memories. I come from the provincial Australian city of Launceston, Tasmania, where home baking was a part of family life. My mother was and still is a good home cook. Food was healthy and nutritious without being overindulgent.

Sunday mornings were spent delivering scones to the neighbours with a pot of homemade jam; today, at 74, my mother still maintains this family tradition. For those of us who made it out of bed on time the reward was hot buttered scones, milk and coffee (and no dishes if you timed it right!). Scones were the first thing I learnt to cook, cautioned by Mum's standard phrase, "If you are going to cook you'll have to clean up your mess."

Mum always had time to teach me, which brings back wonderful memories of baking successes and failures: like the day I made my first loaf of bread and put it in the warming drawer to rise, only to find out I had baked it on top and left uncooked gunk underneath, or the coconut ice I so proudly made with water not milk. However, it was the amount of sherry to add to the Gofton trifle that is one of my best memories. I think it was my dad who instructed me in that area! I had two uncles, George and Rex, who travelled widely and filled me with wonder with stories of their travels and the foods of Spain where they spent most of their time.

There was always discussion about what made good food and wine at collective family meals, and my appetite for learning more about food was fuelled by this frequent debate. Food has become my life, but baking remains my passion. There is nothing quite like walking into a house where the wafting aroma of baking is floating out of the kitchen — even the strongest of wills find it hard to resist a sample. Whether it is tin fillers for the family's lunch boxes, muffins for a late Sunday brunch, or a special cake or dessert, there is immense satisfaction gained from being creative and preparing good food for special friends or family.

With all the health messages today about diet, we are often at war with ourselves as to what is 'good' or 'bad'. Having worked within the health promotion industry for some years, I am concerned that we no longer enjoy the food on our plate but rather count the calories. Baking is about enjoyment and moderation. It is not about feeling guilty or never having a hot scone with butter or a pancake with maple syrup. Like all things in life, everything in moderation.

In this collection of my favourite recipes, there will be something that you will enjoy. I have used a food processor predominantly to eliminate the time-consuming hand beating. I realise that many of you may not have a processor or would prefer to use hand methods, so where appropriate I have added these instructions to the base of each recipe.

Even after 12 months of baking every weekend and most week nights, I still enjoy baking. I am writing this introduction last, and as the book comes to an end I have friends for dinner to prepare for. But before that I have a builder and partner to feed, so it's hot savoury scones and soup!

Ingredients

My pantry has been overflowing for months with different ingredients for the book, and while there are occasionally fancy ingredients, this has mostly meant quantities of flour, sugar and other basic baking requirements. The following is a run-down on what ingredients I prefer to cook with that have been used in testing the recipes in this book.

Flour

There are two grades of flour and both are valuable additions to your pantry. I have used Elfin flours for my recipes: Pure Flour for the majority of recipes in the book, and High Grade Flour for breads or fruit cakes. High Grade Flour has a higher protein (gluten) content, and it should be used when strength is required to hold the shape and structure of your baking, for example breads, fruit cakes or puff pastries. Pure flour is great for all other types of baking.

Flour should be stored away from heat so that it does not dry out. This causes staling and alters the liquid to flour ratio of the recipe. Wholemeal flour should be bought when required and not kept for long periods as it will quickly become rancid, particularly in a humid climate. Plain flours that have had the bran removed will not become rancid as quickly. Keep flour in an airtight container away from direct sunlight or excessive warmth.

Sugar

I am a fan of caster sugar because so much of my baking is prepared in the food processor and caster sugar dissolves much quicker. Once we would beat by hand (or with a beater) to produce a cream from butter and sugar, and in doing so dissolve the sugar. In the processor this does not happen as well. To counteract this, the preparation routine is altered. The eggs and sugar are processed first, then the butter is added. This ensures easy and efficient creaming. Caster sugar dissolves much quicker and produces a lighter texture.

Granulated sugar is best used for rubbed-in mixtures, as it will produce a speckled crust with a reduced volume in creamed mixtures.

Raw sugar can be mixed half-and-half on occasions to add taste and texture, though it does not dissolve well and can result in a grainy texture. I would only suggest this for wholemeal slice type baking. I have used Chelsea sugar throughout the book for its consistent high quality and range of sugars available.

Eggs

The size of eggs used can make a very big difference to your baking. I always use size 7. This is the largest size; if you have anything less, you may need to add an extra egg. For example, a size 7 egg = 62 grams; a size 6 egg = 53 grams. If a recipe in my book calls for 6 eggs, you will need 372 grams of eggs. If you use size 6 eggs you will need to have seven size 6 eggs to equal the same gram weight. This can be tricky when you are cooking from overseas magazines as you can never be too sure what size eggs are being used.

Eggs should always be at room temperature before baking.

Vanilla essence

For all the experts that say that there is no difference between vanilla essence and vanilla extract, I maintain they're wrong. Pure vanilla has a much more subtle flavour and adds a more refined taste to food. Imitation vanilla essence or extract comes mainly from by-products of the paper industry and leaves a bitter aftertaste. Use pure vanilla essence where you can. I always have a canister of vanilla sugar on hand and an extra couple of vanilla pods. Do not buy vanilla sugar, as it is terribly expensive. To make your own, add a vanilla pod to a canister of sugar (caster or granulated) and leave for two weeks before using. The sugar will subtly scent all your baking.

Butter

I have to admit I am known for my love of butter. This is because I believe it has a superior taste to margarine. (And for that statement I am eternally apologetic to all my friends in the 'yellow fats margarine' industry.) This is not to say margarine will not cook well in baking (it does very well), I just prefer the flavour of butter.

Butter should always be kept in an airtight container as it will taint quickly with other fridge odours, especially if you have left it near something oniony!

Use unsalted butter for fine desserts and pastries as it will enhance the flavour of the dish.

Nuts

The nuts we buy here are often already rancid. They sit in a warm warehouse before being placed on the shelves of a warm supermarket, and then they may sit in the pantry for some time before they are used. No wonder they are not fresh: all nuts have oil in them and kept in a warm environment they will go rancid. Buy nuts where there is a good turnover of product. I have mostly used nuts from Tasti (a New Zealand company) in this book, and have been happy with them. As soon as they are bought I put them straight in the freezer.

Lightly toasting nuts will certainly enhance the flavour of a dish, but do not process nuts while they are warm as they will form a paste as opposed to being finely ground.

If you are grinding your own nuts and require 1 cup ground, begin with 1¼ cups of whole nuts and pulse to obtain an even ground texture.

Chocolate

We do not have ready access to coverture chocolate, which has a much finer flavour. In the main the baking chocolate on the market tends to be overpowering and lack flavour. If you can get hold of good quality chocolate, use it.

Store chocolate well wrapped in an airtight container away from dampness and strong odours, as it will absorb strong flavours.

Raising agents

Baking powder is a mixture of cream of tartar and baking soda in a ratio of one part baking soda to two parts cream of tartar, and has a little starch or flour added to stabilize the mixture and prevent caking. It does not keep forever, losing its strength once it is over 12 months old.

Dried fruit

Currants, raisins and sultanas are all dried grapes of different varieties. Currants are small black seedless grapes, seedless raisins are a larger variety, sultanas are small white seedless grapes, while dessert raisins are large muscatel grapes that really need to be stoned before cooking. To me, these have the best flavour. When buying dried fruit always look for plump juicy fruit that does not look dried out or wizened. Store it in airtight containers to maintain freshness. If fruit does become too hard from long storage, soak it in hot water for a short while and then dry on absorbent paper.

Substitutions

It happens to all of us. You decide to make something on the spur of the moment, get halfway through the recipe and find you don't have something. These are a few substitutions that you can make. They will give acceptable results, though not always the same as the original recipe.

Light brown sugar: for every 1 cup of light brown sugar use 1 cup sugar plus ¼ cup treacle or golden syrup.
Dark brown sugar: for every 1 cup dark brown sugar use 1 cup sugar plus ½ cup treacle or golden syrup.
1 tblsp fresh yeast: 2¼ tsp or 1 envelope dried yeast.
1 cup caster sugar: process 1 cup plus 2 tblsp granulated sugar in a food processor for about 1 minute until fine.

Buttermilk: for every 1 cup required use 1 cup plain non-fat yoghurt, or 1 cup milk with 1 tblsp lemon juice or white vinegar mixed into it left to stand for 5 minutes.

Baking powder: for every 1 teaspoon required you can substitute ¼ tsp baking soda plus ½ cup buttermilk or sour milk and reduce the liquid in the recipe by ½ cup.

Baking powder: make up with 2 tsp cream of tartar and 1 teaspoon baking soda. Add a pinch of cornflour if storing. This will help prevent caking.

Self rising flour: for every 1 cup plain flour add 1½ tsp baking powder plus a good pinch of salt.

Butter: for 250 grams use the same quantity in margarine or ⅞ cup oil.

Coconut (desiccated): for every cup of desiccated coconut use 1¼ cups flaked.

Corn syrup: for every 1 cup of corn syrup use 1¼ cups packed brown sugar plus ¼ cup of the same liquid called for in the recipe.

Egg (whole): for 1 egg you can substitute 2 egg yolks plus 1 tablespoon water if you have an abundance of egg yolks in the house.

Honey: for 1 cup of honey use 1¼ cups sugar plus ¼ cup of the same liquid used in the recipe.

Lemon juice: 1 teaspoon lemon juice is equivalent to ½ teaspoon vinegar (preferably white).

Milk (blue): 1 cup non-fat milk plus 2 tablespoons butter or margarine; or ½ cup water and ½ cup evaporated milk; or 1 cup soy milk; or ½ cup cream and ½ cup water.

To process or beat

That really is the big question. Can you achieve good results using a food processor, as opposed to the way our mothers used to bake? Most of my cooking is done with the food processor. In fact I am not sure how I would cope today without a good food processor. I do not use it for everything, though when I am making up batches of soup, baking more than two things, or just generally doing more than one thing in the kitchen, I look to the food processor to make my life easier.

I have had my Cuisinart for about four years now and I would not swap it. All the recipes cooked in this book were tested in that machine and more than once in most instances. I am very vocal about telling people to buy a good food processor. By this I mean one that will make bread, mince, crush ice, and purée a decent quantity. All too often the middle-of-the range machines do not come up to scratch and they cut out just when everything is a walloping great mess. Then you have to dig everything out and make it up by hand. Invest in a good machine; it will be a great asset in your kitchen.

As to whether you can bake better by using one? In essence you can do just as well. Unlike hand beating, if you prepare the creaming base to a baking recipe in the processor, you cannot incorporate much air into the mixture. After all, the food processor is a closed unit and air cannot get in. Also, unless you alter the method you will end up with a lump of butter under the blades. To answer these two issues always beat the eggs and sugar first until light, about 2-3 minutes, and then add the softened butter and process until the mixture is light and creamy, about a further 1–3 minutes.

Folding in flour should be a gentle action, so pulse in the flour. Never let the motor run or your cake will be like rubber.

If you have tender ingredients to mix in such as corn flakes or dried fruits, layer the ingredients in order to keep them whole without being mulched by the blade. I begin with the flour, then add the liquid and then the tender stuff and pulse only until just mixed — no more. Follow this procedure, which I use all the time, and you can make very good cakes in your food processor.

Emergency disguises

Accidents. We all have them! Next time something goes wrong, don't panic. See if you can disguise the result, or use the finished product another way. The ingredients are expensive and so often only you know it hasn't worked properly.

- If your cake has peaked, slice the top off, turn it over, and decorate the bottom of the cake.
- If the cake has sunk in the middle, turn it out, cut a hole in the middle, ice and serve as a ring cake. Or you could put fresh fruit in the centre.
- If a cake has turned out spongy or soggy, serve it warm with custard as a dessert.
- Crumbly biscuits can be processed and used to make the base for a dessert.
- If the top of your cake burns, slice it off and ice.
- If the cake is dry, soak it well with alcohol or fruit juice. Or, crumb and make into rum balls.

Equipment and preparation

Cake tins

Choose good-quality cake tins and baking equipment; that way they will last well. I prefer non-stick cake tins as they clean easily and, when looked after and used properly, enable you to turn out baking without any problems. Once they become scratched and dented, they will be like any others.

Sizes

Use the size specified in the recipe. A tin size change either way will result in a different end result. Too small a tin and the mixture will expand and collapse before baking, with the excess pouring over the edge onto your oven floor, too big a tin and you could end up with a slice not a cake.

Substituting shapes

If you want to choose a cake tin that is a different shape but still the same size, say swap a heart for a round, then use one with the same liquid capacity. Test this by filling the tins to the brim with water.

Preparation

I was brought up to grease cake tins well, but I cannot help thinking it must be difficult for a cake to grab hold of the greased sides and rise evenly. It would be like trying to hang onto a slippery pole! For this reason I always grease, flour and line: lightly grease the tin and then sprinkle in a little flour. Tap the tin, turning around to ensure an even coverage, and then shake out the excess so that only a fine dust of flour covers the tin all over. Cut a piece of baking paper to fit the base of the cake tin. This will ensure that the cake or loaf will turn out without any frustration or disappointment.

The basics

If you are just starting out baking for your home it is nice to have several sized tins to choose from. These are the main ones to have:

- Muffin tray
- Baking tray
- Slice tin
- Round 20 cm cake tin (preferably with interchangeable base to become a ring tin)
- Loaf or bread tin (preferably two)
- Square 20 cm cake tin (can double for slices)
- Flan tin (loose based)

It is best to buy loose-bottomed round tins, as they are marvellous to work with.

Ovens

The single most important factor in producing a successful baked product is your oven temperature. I understand we all get to 'know' our ovens and can judge the way they cook. However, I cannot overstate the importance of having your oven thermostat checked to ensure that the temperature is exactly what it says. Old ovens do vary from new ones, and if you are constantly having problems then maybe your oven is worth checking.

Always pre-heat your oven to the stated temperature; never put cakes into a cold oven.

If you are cooking more than one thing at a time, use the fan option if you have one and allow sufficient room for the flow of air between the tins.

If you cook a basic cake recipe, such as the Buttermilk Cake, for the stated time you can gauge if your oven's temperature is right by the cake's appearance. If it has peaked and is cooked ahead of time your oven is too hot; if it sinks slightly and takes much longer, your oven is too cool. Have it checked either way.

General kitchen tools for baking

The following is a list of equipment that is good to have on hand for baking (and general cooking too).

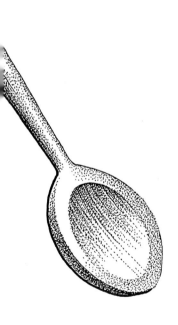

- Standard New Zealand cup measures. The sets are readily available. Only 1 cup, ½ cup and ¼ cup measures are used in this book.
- Pyrex measuring jugs with liquid level markings. Pyrex will withstand heat and handles that can be poured from easily help prevent any disasters when hot liquid is involved.
- New Zealand standard measuring spoons with 1 tablespoon, 1 teaspoon, ½ teaspoon and ¼ teaspoon measures. In New Zealand the tablespoon is equivalent to 3 teaspoons; in Australia it is 4.
- Sieve for sifting flour or straining liquids.
- Glazing brushes. Have two, a wide one and a standard one. Do buy good ones, avoiding cheap nylon bristles as they are often too firm. Try to keep one for greasing only, save the other for all other activities.
- Grater with coarse and fine teeth for grating chocolates or rinds from citrus fruits.
- Cake racks to cool on. Preferably the racks marked into squares as they have more support than those with just bars.
- Spatulas for scraping. Buy decent ones that will last and withstand the hot water in the dishwasher if you have one. Cheap ones will perish quickly.

- Wooden spoons for mixing. Always keep them clean and preferably keep them separate from those you use for savoury cooking such as pickles.
- Palate knife for icing the top of a cake or slice smoothly.
- Set of bowls. I have Decor plastic bowls and 2 Mason and Cash bowls, which I have had for years, and they are all still going well.
- Whisk for beating and whipping cream.
- Hand-held beaters are sufficient for making good cakes if you do not have a large 'mix master'.

Things that are nice to have but not necessary:

- Food processor (I maintain this is one of the best things to buy first.) However, with a wooden spoon or a hand-held beater and elbow grease you can make anything.
- Zesters for citrus rind (but you can use a peeler and slice finely).
- A cherry stoner, though an old-fashioned hairpin will suffice.
- An icing bag with nozzles.
- Double saucepan, though in its place you can use a pyrex bowl and a saucepan.

Always wash equipment and dry well to avoid rust.

1. All spoon and cup measures are level unless otherwise stated. Sets of metric measuring spoons and cups are available at all cookery shops and in most supermarkets.
2. Ovens should always be pre-heated to the cooking temperature required. Grills should also be pre-heated.
3. Butter has been used throughout, though good quality margarine can be substituted.
4. Size 7 eggs have been used throughout.
5. Measure flour by spooning flour into a measuring cup and levelling off. If you dip a cup into the flour and pack it firmly, there will be more flour than the recipe calls for.
6. Measure liquids at eye level, preferably sitting the measuring cup or jug on a bench.

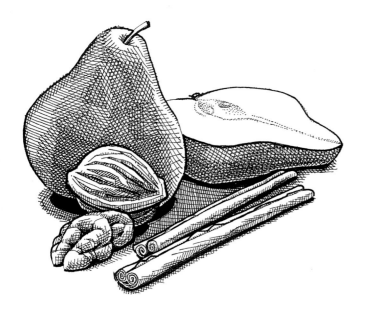

Opposite (from top to bottom): Dutch Ginger Slice (page 18), Chocolate Walnut Slice (page 24), Laurice's Fruit Slice (page 18), Cashew Fruit Bars (page 23), Peppermint Chocolate Crunch (page 19), Caramel Squares (page 30)

SLICES

Next to scones, slices or 'tray cookies' as we called them, were my first introduction to baking. I am sure this was because my mother felt my ability to make not only a mess but a disaster was minimised, therefore making the prospect of success relatively high! In particular I remember Peppermint Chocolate Crunch. I first cooked this recipe at school in Tasmania, at the age of about 13, and it is now engraved in my mind. Over the years the level of cocoa has increased with my love of chocolate, and my weight has gone up in direct proportion to this! Today, my resistance to Peppermint Chocolate Crunch remains low.

Slices vary from rich and sumptuous to oaty and healthful, and they are easy to make. They are ideal for children learning to cook, as the high success rate generates a great deal of satisfaction.

There's plenty here to try — don't forget the Peppermint Chocolate Crunch!

Opposite: White Chocolate Brownies (page 37).

Dutch ginger slice

16 pieces

Cook's Tip:

Use vanilla caster sugar to increase the flavour of this recipe. To make vanilla caster sugar place one vanilla pod into a jar of caster sugar. The longer the sugar is in contact with the vanilla pod, the more intense the flavour. Replenish the sugar as you use it.

My Uncle George in Tasmania is 80 years old and he still cooks every day, making bread for himself and his neighbours. This fabulous slice is one of my favourites from his repertoire and whenever I go home, there is a batch waiting for me.

2 cups pure flour	*1 cup finely chopped crystallized ginger*
1 tsp baking powder	*1 cup soft unsalted butter*
½ tsp salt	*1 egg*
¾ cup caster sugar	*little extra caster sugar*

1. Sift the flour, baking powder, salt and sugar into a bowl. Stir in ¾ of the ginger.
2. Add the softened butter and mix with a wooden spoon to form a soft dough. Beat in the egg.
3. Press into a well greased, floured and lined 23 cm round cake tin and sprinkle the remaining ginger on top.
4. Bake at 180°C for 40 minutes.
5. Cool in the tin for 10 minutes before turning out onto a cake rack to cool. Dust with extra caster sugar and cut into wedges to serve. You can make the size of the wedge to your own liking. Store in an airtight container.

Laurice's fruit slice

30 pieces

Laurice always serves hers lightly iced with lemon icing.

Laurice is the mother of a girlfriend who I met years ago when I was an exchange student at school in Eltham, Taranaki. My girlfriend now lives in Tasmania and I live here! This recipe works very well and is one I can't resist.

100 grams butter	*1 cup coconut*
1 tblsp golden syrup	*1 cup mixed fruit*
¾ cup caster sugar	*½ tsp vanilla essence*
1 egg	*icing sugar to dust with*
1 cup self rising flour	

1. In a saucepan, melt the butter, golden syrup and caster sugar. Cool.
2. Add the egg and beat well.
3. Stir in the flour, coconut, mixed fruit and vanilla essence.
4. Spread into a greased and paper-lined 20 cm × 30 cm slice tin.
5. Bake at 160°C for 25-30 minutes until cooked.
6. Allow to cool in the tin for 10 minutes. Dust with icing sugar and cut into slices or squares. Store in an airtight container.

Variation:
Add 1 tsp grated orange rind and substitute mixed peel for the dried fruit.

I learnt to make this recipe at Brooks High School in Launceston, Tasmania. It is still one of my all-time favourites and has never failed.

1½ cups pure flour	*3 cups corn flakes*
¼ cup cocoa	*1 cup melted butter*
1½ cups brown sugar	*1 tsp vanilla essence*
1 cup coconut	*extra coconut for garnish*

Peppermint Icing

1½ cups icing sugar
1 tblsp melted butter
peppermint essence to taste
hot water

Chocolate Icing

1½ cups icing sugar
2 tblsp cocoa
1 tblsp melted butter
hot water

Peppermint chocolate crunch

30 slices

1. Sift the flour and cocoa into a bowl.
2. Stir in the brown sugar, coconut and corn flakes and make a well in the centre.
3. Stir in the melted butter and vanilla essence and mix well.
4. Press mixture into a greased, floured and lined 33 cm × 23 cm slice tin.
5. Bake at 180°C for 25 minutes.
6. Cool in the tin for 10 minutes before spreading the peppermint icing over the base. Allow to cool completely before carefully spreading the chocolate icing on top. Sprinkle with coconut. Store in an airtight container.

Icings

Mix the dry ingredients together with the butter. Add sufficient hot water to make an icing of thick spreading consistency. Flavour the peppermint icing as preferred.

Variation:

You can use Weet-Bix instead of corn flakes, but as they are drier you may find that you will need a little more butter or the mixture will be crumbly.

Cook's Tip:

Keep baked goods separately in airtight containers as biscuits or crispy slices will soften if left beside soft cakes.

Apricot squares

30 pieces

1 cup wholemeal flour
125 grams butter

¼ cup sugar
grated rind 1 lemon

Topping

1 cup dried apricots
2 eggs
½ cup brown sugar

½ cup self rising flour
¼ cup chopped walnuts
½ tsp vanilla essence

1. Put the flour, butter, sugar and lemon rind into a food processor and process until the mixture forms moist balls of dough.
2. Press into the base of a greased, floured and lined 24 cm × 30 cm slice tin.
3. Bake at 180°C for 10 minutes.
4. Spread the topping over the shortbread. Return to the oven and bake a further 30 minutes until the topping is set.
5. Cut into squares when cold. Store in an airtight container.

Topping

Dice the apricots and put into a saucepan with sufficient water to cover the fruit. Simmer 10 minutes then drain well. Beat the eggs and brown sugar together until the mixture is light and fluffy. Add the flour, apricots, walnuts and vanilla essence.

Variations:

Use other dried fruits such as prunes or papaya, or even mixed dried fruit.

Cook's Tip:

Pastry that is processed until it forms a ball in the food processor will be tough when cooked. Pulse or process until the dough begins to form small moist balls of dough that will come together when gathered in the hand.

If you do not have wholemeal flour, use plain flour. Great lunch-box filler for kids.

Golden crunch slice

30 pieces

2 cups self rising flour
2 tblsp cocoa
2 cups coconut
3 cups crushed corn flakes

1 cup sugar
250 grams butter
¼ cup golden syrup
1 tsp vanilla essence

Icing

1 cup icing sugar
3 tblsp cocoa
1 tblsp melted butter

1. Sift the flour and cocoa together into a large bowl.
2. Add the coconut, corn flakes and sugar.
3. Melt the butter, mix together with the golden syrup and vanilla essence. Stir into the dry ingredients and mix well.
4. Press into a well greased, floured and lined 24 cm × 30 cm slice tin.
5. Bake at 180°C for 20 minutes.
6. Cover the slice with the chocolate icing while still warm. Cut into slices when cool but not thoroughly cold. Decorate the top with chocolate hail if wished. Store in an airtight container.

Icing

Sift the icing sugar and cocoa into a bowl. Stir in melted butter and sufficient hot water to make an icing of thick consistency.

Variations:

Add grated orange rind to the base and ice with orange butter icing to make a jaffa-style slice.

Lemon slice

24 pieces

Oat bran adds a wonderful nutty taste to this slice.

125 grams butter
½ cup brown sugar
1 cup self rising flour

½ cup coconut
½ cup oat bran

Icing

1 cup icing sugar
1 tblsp soft butter

1 tsp grated lemon rind
hot water

1. Melt the butter.
2. Mix the butter, sugar, flour, coconut and oat bran together.
3. Press into a greased, floured and lined 19 cm × 24 cm slice tin.
4. Bake at 180°C for 20 minutes or until golden. Cool in the tin for 10 minutes before turning out onto a cake rack to cool.
5. Spread the icing over the slice when slightly warm.
6. Cut into slices when cool but not cold. Store in an airtight container.

Icing

Mix the icing sugar, butter and lemon rind together with sufficient hot water to make a thick icing.

Cook's Tip:

To get lemon rind off the grater quickly, use a glazing brush to brush any remaining rind from the grater.

Hinkler squares

30 pieces

These are similar to flapjacks, which were a favourite in a flat I lived in in Worcester, England. They are as scrumptious now as they were then.

1 cup sugar
2½ cups coconut
2½ cups rolled oats
250 grams melted butter

1. In a bowl mix together the sugar, coconut and rolled oats.
2. Pour in the melted butter and stir to mix well.
3. Press into a greased, floured and lined 24 cm × 30 cm slice tin.
4. Bake at 160°C for 25 minutes.
5. Cut into squares while still warm. Store in an airtight container.

Oats — there are so many to choose from. Use either wholegrain or rolled oats.

Muesli chews

16 pieces

½ cup wholemeal flour
½ cup rolled oats
½ cup wheatgerm
50 grams finely chopped dried apricots
½ cup sultanas or dried fruit
¼ cup sunflower seeds

1 tblsp treacle or golden syrup
2 tblsp honey
2 tblsp vegetable oil
150 grams butter
2 tsp vanilla essence
50 grams brown sugar

1. In a bowl mix together the flour, rolled oats, wheatgerm, apricots, sultanas or dried fruit, and sunflower seeds.
2. In a saucepan put the treacle or golden syrup, honey, vegetable oil, butter, vanilla and brown sugar, and heat together only until the butter has melted.
3. Mix the liquid ingredients into the dry ingredients. The mixture will come together to form coarse crumbs.
4. Press the mixture into a well greased, floured and lined 20 cm square cake tin.
5. Bake at 170°C for 30 minutes or until the slice is firm to the touch and golden brown on top.
6. Cool on a wire rack and cut into bars while still warm. Store in an airtight container.

Tangy slices

16 pieces

1 cup self rising wholemeal flour
¼ cup wheatgerm
¼ cup raw sugar

2 tblsp oat bran
100 grams butter

Topping
175 grams brown sugar
½ cup self rising wholemeal flour

grated rind and juice of 2 lemons
2 eggs beaten

All the essential oils are in the orange part of the rind. The white part, or pith, is bitter, so grate the rinds on citrus fruits carefully.

1. In a food processor put the wholemeal flour, wheatgerm, sugar, oat bran and butter. Process until the mixture resembles coarse crumbs.
2. Press the mixture into a greased, floured and lined 23 cm square cake tin.
3. Bake at 180°C for 20 minutes.
4. Pour the topping ingredients over the base and return it to the oven for a further 30 minutes or until the topping is golden brown and firm.
5. Cool in the tin for 20 minutes before turning out onto a cake rack to cool. Cut into bars when cold. Store in an airtight container.

Topping
In a bowl put the sugar, flour, lemon rind and juice, and eggs. Beat well with a wooden spoon until smooth.

Variation:
Add coconut to the base in place of the oat bran.

Cashew nuts are really delicious. Toast them slightly before adding to the topping for this recipe to give an even nuttier taste.

1 cup wholemeal flour
75 grams butter

¼ cup brown sugar
¼ cup oat bran

Topping

2 eggs
½ cup brown sugar
1 tsp vanilla or lemon essence
½ cup self rising wholemeal flour
4 digestive biscuits, crushed

2 × 70-gram pkt cashew nuts
  (chopped)
½ cup sultanas
1 tblsp lemon juice

1. Put the flour, butter, sugar and oat bran into a food processor and process until the mixture resembles coarse crumbs.
2. Press the mixture into a greased, floured and lined 23 cm square cake tin and press down firmly with the back of a spoon.
3. Bake at 180°C for 20 minutes.
4. Pour the topping over and return to the oven for a further 30 minutes.
5. Cool in the tin before cutting into bars while slightly warm. Store in an airtight container.

Topping

Beat the eggs, sugar and vanilla or lemon essence together in a food processor. Pulse in the flour, crushed biscuits, cashew nuts, sultanas and lemon juice.

Cashew fruit bars

20 pieces

Try peanuts or hazelnuts or even a combination for a change.

1 cup rolled oats
1 cup Ricies
4 Weet-Bix crushed
1 cup coconut
½ cup mixed fruit or sultanas

½ cup pure flour
½ cup brown sugar
½ cup honey
½ cup peanut butter
125 grams butter

1. In a large bowl mix together the rolled oats, Ricies, crushed Weet-Bix, coconut, mixed fruit, and flour.
2. In a saucepan heat together the brown sugar, honey, peanut butter, and butter and stir until the sugar has dissolved. Stir over a high heat for 5 minutes until the mixture is thick and caramel in colour.
3. Pour the caramel mixture onto the dry ingredients and stir well.
4. Press the mixture into a greased, floured and lined 24 cm × 30 cm slice tin. Refrigerate overnight before cutting into squares.

Rice bubble and honey slice

30 pieces

Peanut and jelly slice

20 pieces

This will be a great favourite with your children and their friends.

50 grams butter
1 cup self rising flour
2 tblsp rolled oats

2 tblsp sugar
1 egg

Topping

2 eggs
¾ cup caster sugar
25 grams melted butter
2 tblsp raspberry jam

1 cup coconut
50 grams chopped roasted peanuts
  (skins on or off)
1 cup corn flakes

1. Rub the butter into the flour. Stir in the oats and sugar.
2. Beat the egg and stir into the dry ingredients. Mix well.
3. Press the mixture into the base of a greased, floured and lined 23 cm square cake tin.
4. Pour the topping over the base.
5. Bake at 180°C for 30–35 minutes.
6. Cool in the tin before cutting into slices. Store in an airtight container.

Topping

Beat the eggs, sugar, butter and raspberry jam together with a hand held beater or wire whisk until the mixture is thick. Stir in the coconut, peanuts and corn flakes and mix well.

Chocolate walnut slice

30 pieces

Keep this well hidden, it's so absolutely yumptious it will disappear all too fast!

This is a little more time consuming than the other slice recipes included here because there are three separate steps involved. But it is well worth the effort.

Base

175 grams butter
½ tsp vanilla essence
1¼ cups pure flour

½ tsp baking powder
¾ cup brown sugar
1¼ cups rolled oats

Filling

75 grams butter
1 cup caster sugar
¼ cup cocoa
2 eggs
1¾ cups pure flour

½ tsp baking powder
½ tsp vanilla essence
¾ cup chopped walnuts
½ cup milk

Icing

1½ cups icing sugar
2 tblsp cocoa

2 tblsp melted butter
water

1. Melt butter and add vanilla essence.
2. Sift flour and baking powder into a bowl. Stir in sugar and oats. Pour in butter and mix well.
3. Spread base evenly over a greased, floured and lined 24 cm × 30 cm slice tin.
4. Bake at 180°C for 10 minutes.
5. When cool, spread filling evenly over the base.
6. Return to the oven for a further 20 minutes or until cooked. Cool in the tin for 10 minutes.
7. Transfer to a cake rack. Ice when cold. Cut into slices to serve. Store in an airtight container.

Filling:

Melt butter in a saucepan. Put caster sugar and cocoa into a bowl and pour in butter. Add eggs and mix well. Sift flour and baking powder together. Stir into the mixture with the vanilla essence, walnuts and milk.

Icing

Sift icing sugar and cocoa into a bowl. Add butter and sufficient hot water to mix to a smooth icing of spreading consistency.

Apricot wedges

16 wedges

This recipe was prepared for me by a good friend, Ann, who helps me with my work when I am busy. With three children, Ann is well versed in what is a favourite with kids and what is not — this one is definitely a favourite in her home.

½ cup chopped dried apricots	½ tsp mixed spice
¾ cup water	1 tblsp sesame seeds
100 grams butter	2 tblsp sunflower seeds
¾ cup brown sugar	1 tsp baking powder
1½ cups rolled oats	1 egg

1. Simmer the apricots in water until softened — about 10 minutes. Purée in a food processor.
2. Melt the butter and sugar together, stir in rolled oats, mixed spice, sesame seeds and sunflower seeds. Mix well.
3. Add puréed apricots, baking powder and egg — mix only until combined.
4. Divide mixture evenly between two greased, floured and lined 20 cm round cake tins. Press mixture down well.
5. Bake at 180°C for 35 minutes or until golden.
6. Allow to cool in tin before cutting each round into 8 wedges. Store in an airtight container.

Dried apricots seem to be a universal favourite, but try dates, prunes or even mixed fruit.

Date crumble bars

30 pieces

1½ cups chopped dates
1 cup water
½ cup brown sugar
200 grams butter
1 egg
½ tsp vanilla essence
2 cups pure flour

1 cup rolled oats
1 tsp baking powder
pinch salt
1 tsp mixed spice
½ cup coconut
¼ cup extra rolled oats
¼ cup extra pure flour

1. Put the dates and water into a saucepan with 2 tablespoons of the sugar. Simmer for 3-5 minutes until mushy.
2. Put butter, the remaining brown sugar, egg, and vanilla essence into a food processor and process until well mixed and creamy.
3. Add the 2 cups of flour and 1 cup of the oats, the baking powder, salt, mixed spice and coconut and pulse until just mixed.
4. Spread three-quarters of the mixture over the base of a well greased, floured and lined 20 cm × 30 cm slice tin. Spread dates evenly on top.
5. Add the ¼ cup of extra oats and flour to the remaining mixture, pulse to blend then sprinkle over the date filling and press down.
6. Bake at 180°C for 25-30 minutes.
7. Cut into pieces once cool. Store in an airtight container.

Variation:
Use prunes or even apricots instead of dates.

Munch bar

30 pieces

1 cup oat flakes
1 cup oat bran
1 cup chopped walnuts
½ cup chopped almonds
1 cup evenly chopped dates
½ cup pumpkin seeds
¼ cup non-fat milk powder
½ tsp salt

½ cup pure flour
2 tsp grated orange rind
½ cup brown sugar
1 cup liquid honey
¼ cup oil
75 grams butter
1 tsp vanilla essence

1. Mix together oat flakes, oat bran, walnuts, almonds, dates, pumpkin seeds, milk powder, salt and flour.
2. In a saucepan bring to the boil orange rind, sugar, honey, oil, butter and vanilla essence. Boil for 2 minutes, then stir into the dry ingredients and mix well.
3. Press mixture firmly into a well greased, floured and lined 23 cm × 33 cm slice tin.
4. Bake at 180°C for 30 minutes or until firm to the touch.
5. Sprinkle with sifted icing sugar or spread with a thin layer of lemon icing. Allow to cool before cutting into slices. Store in an airtight container.

Butterscotch doesn't seem to be a well-promoted flavour. I like it a lot, and this slice is really delicious.

150 grams butter
1 cup brown sugar
1 tsp vanilla essence
1 egg

1½ cups pure flour
2 tsp baking powder
1 tsp mixed spice
1½ cups mixed dried fruit

Butterscotch icing

50 grams butter
¼ cup brown sugar
1 cup icing sugar
1 tblsp cream or milk

1. Melt the butter with the brown sugar and vanilla essence over a low heat, stirring constantly.
2. Remove from the heat, allow to cool, then beat in egg.
3. Sift flour, baking powder and mixed spice together.
4. Toss the dried fruit through the dry ingredients.
5. Stir the flour and fruit into the butter mixture.
6. Spread into a greased, floured and lined 24 cm × 30 cm slice tin.
7. Bake at 180°C for 15 minutes, or until firm to touch and golden brown.
8. Ice with butterscotch icing while hot. When cold, cut into slices. Store in an airtight container.

Butterscotch icing
Heat butter and brown sugar together in a small saucepan until butter has melted. Add icing sugar and stir to mix. Add cream or milk and beat until smooth.

Variation:
Use half finely chopped nuts and mixed fruit in place of all dried fruit and change the spices to suit. Nutmeg is nice with butterscotch.

Butterscotch slice

30 slices

Try sultanas or mixed peel too.

Louise slice

30 pieces

I'm not sure of the origin of Louise Slice, or Louise Cake as it is often called, but it is a New Zealand favourite and a baking book wouldn't be complete without a recipe for it. I have made it with half wholemeal flour to add a nutty flavour and some health.

100 grams butter	2 tblsp milk
¼ cup caster sugar	½ cup red jam (raspberry, plum or
3 eggs, separated	currant)
1 tsp vanilla essence	¾ cup caster sugar
1 cup self rising flour	¾ cup coconut
1 cup wholemeal self rising flour	

1. Put the butter, first measure of sugar, egg yolks and vanilla essence into a food processor and process until well mixed.
2. Add the flours and the milk and process to combine.
3. Spread the mixture into a greased, floured and lined 24 cm × 30 cm slice tin.
4. Spread with red jam.
5. In a clean bowl whisk the egg whites until stiff but not dry. Add the second measure of caster sugar and beat until thick. Fold in the coconut. Spread over the slice.
6. Bake at 180°C for 25–30 minutes.
7. Cool and slice into squares. Store in an airtight container.

Variation:
Use apricot jam, and add ¼ cup chopped dried apricots or peel to the jam as well.

Quick lemon squares

30 pieces

¼ cup oat bran	½ cup chopped walnuts
1½ cups self rising flour	200 grams butter
½ cup sugar	2 tblsp golden syrup
½ cup coconut	grated rind 1 lemon
4 Weet-Bix, crushed	

Icing

50 grams butter	grated rind 1 lemon
1½ cups icing sugar	juice 1 lemon

1. In a bowl mix together the oat bran, flour, sugar, coconut, Weet-Bix and walnuts.
2. Melt the butter and add to the dry ingredients with the golden syrup and lemon rind. Mix well.
3. Press the mixture into a greased, floured and lined 24 cm × 30 cm slice tin.

4. Bake at 180°C for 25 minutes.
5. Ice when cool. Cut into squares. Store in an airtight container.

Icing

Beat together the butter, icing sugar, lemon rind and juice to a spreading consistency. Add water if necessary.

Ginger slice

30 slices

This is my version of the ever-popular Ginger Crunch. I have included oat bran for a nuttier taste and the icing is much creamier than the usual one. I hope you like it.

175 grams butter
¾ cup sugar
1½ cups self rising flour

½ cup oat bran
2 tsp ground ginger

Icing

75 grams butter
1 tblsp golden syrup

2 tsp ground ginger
1½ cups icing sugar

1. Put the butter and sugar into a food processor and process until well mixed.
2. Add the flour, oat bran and ground ginger and pulse to mix.
3. Press the mixture into a greased, floured and lined 24 cm × 30 cm slice tin.
4. Bake at 180°C for 25 minutes.
5. Remove from the oven and cool. Spread with the icing when cool. Cut into slices. Store in an airtight container.

Add extra tang with lemon rind in the icing or base.

Icing

Beat together the butter, golden syrup and ground ginger until smooth. Add the icing sugar and beat well, adding a little water until the mixture is spreadable.

Variation:

Use wholemeal flour in place of the plain.

By hand:

Sift the dry ingredients into a bowl. Stir in the oat bran. Rub in the butter until the mixture resembles coarse crumbs. Continue from step 3.

T.V. slice

30 pieces

250 grams butter
½ cup sugar
1 egg

1 cup self rising flour
½ cup coconut

Topping

1 cup icing sugar
3 tblsp condensed milk
1 cup coconut

1 tblsp butter
1 tblsp cocoa

This recipe comes from a fund-raising book prepared for our local Golf Club near where I grew up. Try adding grated rind of an orange to the base.

1. Beat the butter, sugar and egg together in a food processor until light and creamy.
2. Pulse in the flour and coconut.
3. Press the base into a greased, floured and lined 24 cm × 30 cm slice tin.
4. Spread the topping evenly over the base.
5. Bake at 180°C for 15-20 minutes until cooked.
6. Cut into slices when cold. Store in an airtight container.

Topping

Warm the icing sugar, condensed milk, coconut, butter and cocoa together in a saucepan and stir to mix well.

Hand beater method:

You can prepare the base by beating the butter and sugar together until light. Add the egg and then fold in the sifted flour and coconut.

Caramel squares

30 pieces

These are indulgent, so I have added wholemeal flour and corn flakes. Use all plain flour if you wish.

75 grams butter
½ cup sugar
1 egg

½ cup self rising wholemeal flour
½ cup pure flour
¼ cup custard powder

Caramel

25 grams butter
397-gram tin condensed milk

2 tblsp golden syrup
½ tsp vanilla essence

Topping

1 cup coconut
½ cup sugar
1 cup crushed corn flakes

¼ cup pure flour
25 grams butter
1 egg

1. Put the butter, sugar and egg into a food processor and process until well mixed.
2. Add the flours and custard powder and pulse to mix well.
3. Press the dough into the base of a greased, floured and lined 20 cm × 30 cm slice tin.

4. Spread the cooled caramel mixture on top and carefully dot the topping over. The topping will join as it cooks.
5. Bake at 180°C for 25 minutes. Store in an airtight container.
6. Cut into squares when cold.

Caramel

Put the butter, condensed milk, golden syrup and vanilla essence into a small saucepan and cook over a moderate heat, stirring constantly for 3 minutes until the mixture has thickened and become caramel-like.

Topping

In a bowl, combine the coconut, sugar, crushed corn flakes and flour. Melt the butter and mix with the egg into the dry ingredients.

By hand:

Beat the butter and sugar to a cream. Add the egg and beat well. Mix in the sifted dry ingredients. Continue from step 3.

Apricot muesli bars

24-30 pieces

This recipe was designed by colleague Pauline Willoughby and is particularly popular with her girls, Catherine and Louise. It's a great recipe for the lunch box.

125 grams butter
¾ cup brown sugar
½ cup honey
½ cup peanut butter
¼ cup finely chopped dried apricots
¼ cup sunflower seeds

2 tblsp sesame seeds
4 Weet-Bix
2 cups Ricies
1 cup rolled oats
1 cup coconut

1. Place butter, brown sugar, honey and peanut butter in a saucepan.
2. Stir over low heat until sugar is dissolved. Bring to the boil, reduce heat and simmer 5 minutes while stirring often.
3. Remove from heat and add dried apricots, sunflower seeds and sesame seeds. Set aside to cool a little.
4. Crush Weet-Bix. Place Weet-Bix, Ricies, rolled oats and coconut in a large bowl. Add honey mixture and stir until combined.
5. Press into greased 30 cm × 20 cm slice tin. Refrigerate until firm and then cut into bars.

Cook's Tip:

- *Try mixed peel, finely sliced prunes or dried pineapple instead of apricots.*
- *Try chopped peanuts, walnuts or pumpkin seeds instead of sunflower seeds.*
- *Use crunchy or smooth peanut butter.*

Crunchy sultana slice

30 pieces

Corn flakes are one cereal found in many pantries. They're useful in cooking too. Try this one, it's a great lunch-box filler.

175 grams butter
½ tsp vanilla essence
1 egg
1½ cup crushed corn flakes

1 cup sugar
1½ cup self rising flour
1 cup sultanas

Icing
1 cup icing sugar
2 tblsp melted butter
grated rind 1 orange

1. Melt the butter and stir in the vanilla essence. Add the egg and beat well.
2. In a bowl mix together the corn flakes, sugar, flour and sultanas. Stir in the butter mixture.
3. Press into a greased, floured and lined 20 cm × 30 cm slice tin.
4. Bake at 180°C for 30 minutes.
5. Ice while warm and cut into bars when cold.

Icing
Mix icing sugar with melted butter, the orange rind and sufficient hot water to make an icing of thick consistency.

Chocolate coconut slice

30 pieces

A one-bowl mix. Let your children have a crack at this.

1½ cups self rising flour
1 cup sugar
1½ cups coconut

2 tblsp cocoa
200 grams melted butter
¼ cup grated chocolate or chocolate hail

Icing
1½ cups icing sugar
2 tblsp cocoa
2 tblsp melted butter

Add a few drops of peppermint essence to the icing — kids will love it!

1. Place all in a bowl and mix well. Press into a well greased, floured and lined 24 cm × 30 cm slice tin.
2. Bake at 180°C for 15-20 minutes until firm.
3. Ice with chocolate icing and cut into squares while still warm. Store in an airtight tin.

Icing
Mix the icing sugar with the cocoa, melted butter and sufficient hot water to make an icing of thick consistency.

Opposite (from left to right): Ginger Creams (page 42), Honey Biscuits (page 51), Custard Dreams (page 48), Cinnamon Nut Biscuits (page 47), Oatmeal Raisin Biscuits (page 45), Anzacs (page 43), Burnt Butter Biscuits (page 43).

BROWNIES

Dense, chewy and rich in chocolate, brownies have a special place in my recipe collection. One story credits their creation to a librarian called Brownie from Maine in the United States, who forgot to add baking powder to her cake and served it cut in slices as it was!

I hope you will try one of my favourite's — the White Chocolate Brownie (I'm a white chocoholic) or the Mocha Brownie.

If you want a brownie that has a more cakey (as opposed to chewy) texture, cook your brownies for 5-10 minutes longer (depending on size and depth). The recipes given here are all cooked to fudgey stage.

Opposite (from back to front): Jaffa Butter Biscuits (page 53) Lemon Coconut Biscuits (page 40), Afghans (page 49), Rock Cakes (page 53), Melting Moments (page 47), Bobby's Peanut Biscuits (page 54).

Cocoa brownies

16 brownies

Try hazelnuts or even Brazil nuts.

200 grams unsalted butter
6 heaped tblsp cocoa
4 eggs
2 cups brown sugar

1 tsp vanilla essence
1 cup pure flour
½ tsp salt
70-gram pkt walnuts

1. Melt the butter and cocoa together in the top of a double boiler. Cool the mixture to lukewarm.
2. Beat the eggs and sugar together until the mixture is thick and creamy. Beat in the vanilla essence.
3. Beat the eggs into the chocolate butter mixture until it makes a very creamy batter.
4. Sift the flour and salt together. Mix gradually into the batter until well mixed. Stir in the walnuts before all the flour is folded in.
5. Turn the mixture into a greased, floured and lined 20 cm square cake tin.
6. Bake at 180°C for 45–50 minutes. Cool in the tin for 15 minutes.
7. Invert onto a rack and peel off the paper. Cut into squares when cool.

Cook's Tip:

The sugar needs to be dissolved and the eggs and sugar well beaten when making brownies. Food processors do not make good brownies. I've made these with a hand-held beater.

Cake brownies

16 brownies

100 grams unsalted butter
¾ cup caster sugar
1 tsp vanilla essence
4 eggs

¾ cup pure flour
½ tsp salt
2 × 70-gram pkt walnuts
50 grams dark chocolate

1. Beat the butter, sugar and vanilla essence together until light and creamy.
2. Beat in the eggs.
3. Sift the flour and salt together and fold into the creamed mixture with the walnuts.
4. Divide the mixture into two parts. Melt the chocolate and stir into one half of the mixture.
5. Grease, flour and line a 20 cm square cake tin.
6. Drop the batter into the tin in alternate spoonfuls and then run a knife blade through the mixture to obtain a marbled effect.
7. Bake at 180°C for 40 minutes.
8. Let the brownies cool in the cake tin before turning onto a cake rack to cool completely. Cut into squares. Store in an airtight container.

Mocha brownies

24–30 brownies

2 cups brown sugar
¾ cup unsalted butter
2 tblsp instant coffee granules
1 tblsp hot water
2 eggs
2 tblsp vanilla essence

1 cup self rising flour
1 cup pure flour
½ tsp salt
70-gram pkt chopped pecans
1 cup chocolate chips (use small chips)
about ¼ cup icing sugar for dusting

1. Put the brown sugar and butter into a saucepan. Stir with a wooden spoon until the butter has melted.
2. Dissolve the coffee in the hot water and stir in. Allow the mixture to cool to room temperature.
3. With a hand-held beater, beat the eggs and vanilla essence into the cooled mixture until light.
4. Sift the flours and salt together and stir into the butter mixture alternately with the pecans and chocolate chips.
5. Turn the mixture into a greased, floured and lined 23 cm square cake tin.
6. Bake at 180°C for 45–50 minutes or until firm to touch with a little softness in the centre.
7. Cool in the tin before turning out and cutting into squares. Dust with icing sugar to serve. Store in an airtight container.

Butterscotch brownies

24 brownies

100 grams unsalted butter
1 tsp vanilla essence
1 tblsp golden syrup
200 grams brown sugar

2 eggs
1 cup pure flour
½ tsp salt
70-gram pkt walnuts

1. Beat together the butter, vanilla essence, golden syrup, brown sugar and eggs until the mixture is very light and creamy.
2. Sift the flour and salt together and fold into the creamed mixture with the chopped walnuts.
3. Turn the batter into a greased, floured and lined 23 cm square cake tin. Bake at 180°C for 35 minutes or until a skewer inserted comes out clean.
4. Allow to cool in the tin for 20 minutes before turning out.
Cut into squares. Store in an airtight container.

Cook's Tip:

Use unsalted butter when baking — it allows the flavours to come through. This is especially important when cooking with chocolate.

Food processor fudge brownies

24 brownies

100 grams cooking chocolate
1 cup caster sugar
125 grams unsalted butter
4 eggs
2 tsp vanilla essence
¼ tsp salt
¾ cup pure flour
1 cup chopped walnuts or pecans

1. Chop the chocolate roughly and put into a food processor fitted with the metal blade. Process until coarsely chopped.
2. Add the sugar and process one minute or until the chocolate is as fine as the sugar.
3. Add the softened butter and 2 eggs and process for 1 minute. Add the remaining eggs, vanilla and salt and process until the mixture is well creamed.
4. Sift the flour and add to the mixture with the nuts. Pulse to mix.
5. Turn the mixture into a well greased, floured and lined 23 cm square cake tin.
6. Bake at 180°C for about 40 minutes. At this stage the brownie will be moist but an inserted toothpick should come out clean. The mixture will not have begun to move away from the sides. This will produce a fudge brownie.
7. Let the brownies cool in the tin for 5 minutes before turning out onto a rack to cool. Cut into squares. Store in an airtight container.

Classic brownies

40 brownies

Make a double saucepan using a pyrex bowl placed over a small saucepan of simmering water. Make sure the bowl is pyrex though!

Cook's Tip:

Brownies are so rich that I have only iced a couple of recipes. You can use a chocolate butter icing if you wish.

250 grams cooking chocolate
250 grams unsalted butter
5 eggs
1 tblsp vanilla essence
2 tsp almond essence
3 cups caster sugar
3 tblsp instant coffee granules
1¾ cups pure flour
1 cup coarsely chopped walnuts

1. Melt the chocolate and butter in the top of a double saucepan, stirring occasionally just until the mixture is smooth.
2. With an electric mixer beat the eggs, vanilla, almond essence, sugar and instant coffee together in a large bowl for about 10 minutes on full speed until the eggs are light and very voluminous.
3. Blend in the melted chocolate mixture, then carefully fold in the sifted flour and nuts.
4. Pour the mixture into a well greased, floured and lined 25 cm square cake tin. Bake at 180°C for 60 minutes. The batter will be a little uncooked. Cool to room temperature and then place the tin into the refrigerator overnight.
5. Turn the brownie out and cut into squares. The brownies will have a crispy crust on them. Serve dusted with icing sugar. Store in an airtight container.

275 grams white chocolate
250 grams unsalted butter
1 cup caster sugar
4 eggs

1 tblsp vanilla essence
2 cups pure flour
½ tsp salt
1 cup chopped pistachio nuts or pecans

White chocolate brownies

40 brownies

Icing

50 grams white chocolate
½ cup icing sugar
1 tblsp butter

milk
1 tblsp cocoa for dusting

My favourites!

1. Chop the white chocolate roughly and place in the top of a double saucepan with the butter. Heat over boiling water until just melted. This can be done in the microwave, allowing about 2 minutes on high power. Be careful not to overcook the chocolate as it will burn easily.
2. Beat the sugar, eggs and vanilla essence together until the mixture is light and fluffy.
3. Sift the flour and salt together, and stir into the chocolate mixture alternately with the egg mixture. Fold in the pistachio nuts or pecans.
4. Turn mixture into a greased, floured and lined 25 cm square cake tin.
5. Bake at 160°C for 45–50 minutes, until the top is lightly golden but the centre is still a little soft.
6. Remove from the oven and cool to room temperature before refrigerating for 3-4 hours. Remove from the tin, ice and dust with cocoa. Cut into squares. Store in an airtight container.

Icing

Melt the white chocolate and butter together. Stir in sifted icing sugar and sufficient milk to make a smooth thick icing.

Cook's Tip:

If you really want a wonderful rich chocolate, buy 'coverture chocolate'. It is worth the effort and expense when cooking very rich chocolate goodies.

Sour cream brownies

16 brownies

200 grams cooking chocolate
125 grams unsalted butter
2 eggs
1 cup sugar
1 tsp vanilla essence

½ cup pure flour
pinch salt
¼ cup sour cream
70-gram pkt pecans or walnuts

1. Melt the chocolate and butter together in the top of a double saucepan over simmering water. You can also do this in the microwave, allowing 2 minutes on high power. Allow to cool to room temperature.
2. Beat the eggs, sugar and vanilla essence together with a hand-held or electric mixer until the mixture is light and fluffy.
3. Sift the flour and salt together.
4. Fold the chocolate butter mixture and the egg mixture together. Carefully fold in the flour alternately with the sour cream and chopped pecans or walnuts.
5. Pour the batter into a greased, floured and lined 20 cm square cake tin.
6. Bake at 160°C for 35–45 minutes, until a skewer inserted comes out almost clean. The centre should still be a little cakey.
7. Cool on a cake rack for 1 hour before turning out and cutting into squares. Store in an airtight container.

Cook's Tip:

Giving accurate times for melting food together in the microwave is always difficult. So much depends on the temperature of the food: whether it was at room temperature when it was put in or whether it was taken straight from the fridge. The important thing is not to overcook the chocolate. If in doubt, check it regularly, as chocolate will remain in shape even though it has melted and often burnt.

Carob brownies

20 brownies

½ cup melted unsalted butter
¼ cup carob powder
2 eggs
1 cup brown sugar
1 tsp vanilla essence

¼ tsp salt
1 cup self rising flour
½ cup chopped walnuts
½ cup raisins

1. Beat together the melted butter and carob powder until the mixture is free of lumps.
2. Beat in the eggs, sugar and vanilla until thick.
3. Sift the flour and salt together and fold into the mixture alternately with the walnuts and raisins.
4. Pour into a greased, floured and lined 20 cm square cake tin.
5. Bake at 180°C for 25-30 minutes.
6. Cool in the tin for 15 minutes before turning out. Cut into squares when cold and dust with icing sugar to serve.

BISCUITS

Biscuits are much loved by us all. They bring back fond memories of wonderful aromas wafting out from the kitchen, tempting us in to plead for one warm from the tray!

Biscuits are often the first thing children are allowed to make; they are duly proud of their efforts when biscuits like peanut biscuits emerge from the oven looking as good as Mum's. Wow! This chapter is full of my favourite recipes. Many from my Mum, and heaps from friends and relatives both here and at home.

The food processor has made it easy to whip up a batch of biscuits that are far more economical not to mention tastier than many of the store-bought varieties. So keep a tin full of some of these ideas. I have so many 'favourites' from this section, but my first choice is one of the simplest recipes to make and one of the first I ever learnt to cook: Burnt Butter Biscuits — look out for them!

Lemon coconut biscuits

3 dozen biscuits

Try orange or grapefruit rind.

These are great tin fillers!

1½ cups caster sugar
2 eggs
250 grams butter
2 tsp grated lemon rind

1 cup self rising flour
1¼ cups pure flour
2 cups coconut

1. Put the sugar and eggs into a food processor and process for 2 minutes.
2. Add the butter and lemon rind and process a further 2 minutes.
3. Sift the flours and add to the processor with the coconut and pulse only to mix.
4. Place large teaspoonfuls of the mixture on a greased tray. Press down with a fork.
5. Bake at 180°C for 12–15 minutes until golden brown.
6. Transfer to a cake rack to cool. Store in an airtight container.

Hand/electric beater method

Beat the butter and sugar until light and creamy. Add the eggs and lemon rind, and beat well. Sift the flours together and mix with the coconut using a metal spoon. Continue from step 4.

Chocolate mint biscuits

3 dozen biscuits

These biscuits use After Dinner Mints. Try orange flavoured After Dinner chocolates instead for a completely new version.

¾ cup caster sugar
1 egg
125 grams butter
½ tsp vanilla essence

2 cups pure flour
1 tsp baking powder
125 grams After Dinner Mints
(thin variety)

1. Put the sugar and egg into a food processor and process for 2 minutes.
2. Add the softened butter and vanilla essence and process for a further 2 minutes.
3. Sift the flour and baking powder together. Chop the mints up into even small dice.
4. Add the flour and mints and pulse only to mix. Do not over process.
5. Roll tablespoonfuls into balls and place on greased baking trays.
6. Bake at 180°C for 15 minutes.
7. Transfer to a cake rack to cool. Store in an airtight container.

Hand/electric beater method

Beat the butter and sugar until light and creamy. Add the eggs and vanilla essence and beat well. Chop the mints finely and fold into the creamed mixture with the sifted flour and baking powder. Continue from step 5.

Unsalted butter brings out the magical flavour of the orange blossom water and walnuts in these butter biscuits.

Butter biscuits

3 dozen biscuits

¾ cup caster sugar
2 egg yolks
250 grams unsalted butter
1 tsp orange blossom water

2 cups pure flour
pinch salt
¼ cup finely chopped walnuts

1. Put the sugar and egg yolks into a food processor and process for 2 minutes or until light.
2. Add the butter and orange blossom water, and process a further 2 minutes or until the mixture is light and fluffy.
3. Add the sifted flour and salt, and pulse until all the ingredients are well mixed.
4. Roll teaspoonfuls of the mixture into balls and dip the top half into the chopped walnuts. Place on a greased baking tray with the walnut tops upwards, allowing plenty of room for the dough to spread. Use a fork to press the biscuits down.
5. Bake at 180°C for 10-12 minutes.
6. Cool on a cake rack. Store in an airtight container.

Hand/electric beater method

Beat the butter and sugar until creamy. Add the egg yolks and orange blossom water, and beat well. Sift flour and salt together, and mix in with a metal spoon. Continue from step 4.

Variations

- Add ½ cup chocolate chips. You need to have them chopped a bit like shavings as opposed to chunks.
- Omit the orange blossom water and use the grated rind of 1 lemon.
- Omit ¼ cup flour and add ¼ cup cocoa instead.
- Add the finely chopped walnuts to the mixture.

Cook's Tip:

To make cakes and biscuits successfully in a food processor, change the method by mixing the eggs and sugar first followed by the butter.

Ginger creams

2½ dozen biscuits

Ginger is one of my mother's favourite spices, be it in biscuits or puddings. It has been around for ages — ginger that is, not my mother! Ginger was one of the first spices readily available, hence its popularity over the years. Add more to this recipe if it is one of your favourites.

½ cup sugar	2½ cups pure flour
1 egg	1½ tsp baking powder
1 tblsp golden syrup	pinch salt
250 grams softened butter	1 tsp ground ginger

Ginger cream
100 grams butter
1½ cups icing sugar
2 tblsp finely chopped crystallized ginger

You can roll teaspoonful lots into balls and flatten with a fork if you don't have a piping bag.

1. Put the sugar, egg and golden syrup into a food processor and process for 2 minutes until light.
2. Add the softened butter and process for a further 2 minutes until light and creamy.
3. Sift the flour, baking powder, salt and ginger together and sprinkle evenly over the creamed mixture. Pulse to mix well. Do not over process.
4. Put the mixture into a piping bag fitted with a star nozzle and pipe into 5 cm strips on a greased tray.
5. Bake at 180°C for 12–15 minutes until light brown.
6. Transfer to a cake rack to cool. Join the fingers together with ginger cream. Store in an airtight container.

Ginger cream
Beat the butter and icing sugar together until smooth and pale. Fold in the minced or finely chopped ginger.

Hand/electric beater method
Beat the butter and sugar together. Add the egg and golden syrup and beat well. Fold in the sifted flour, ginger, baking powder and salt. Continue from step 4.

Cook's Tip:

The pulse button is used to mix ingredients together. It pushes the ingredients up and then they drop down and move around. Using it repeatedly helps to mix ingredients evenly without turning the mixture into a purée or knocking out all the air from a light mix. Pulse for about 3-4 seconds at a time. Do not hold the pulse button down as if to process, as it will wear your motor out.

So called after the biscuits that were included in the ration packs for the ANZAC soldiers of WWI, these biscuits have always been my dad's favourite. They are quite regularly 'dunked' into tea before munching. They're best that way, so he says!

Anzacs

3 dozen biscuits

1 cup pure flour
pinch salt
1 cup sugar
1 cup rolled oats
125 grams butter

1 tblsp golden syrup
1 tsp vanilla essence
1 tsp baking soda
2 tblsp boiling water

1. Sift the flour and salt together into a large bowl. Stir in the sugar and rolled oats.
2. Melt the butter, golden syrup and vanilla together. Dissolve the baking soda in the boiling water and mix into the flour with the melted butter, stirring until all the ingredients are combined.
3. Roll tablespoonfuls of the mixture into balls and place on greased trays. Flatten lightly with a fork.
4. Bake at 180°C for about 12-15 minutes, until the biscuits have flattened out and become a reddish-brown.
5. Transfer to a cake rack. The biscuits will crispen as they cool. Store in an airtight container.

Cook's Tip:

For a stronger-flavoured Anzac, use treacle in place of golden syrup.

Well, not exactly burnt! These biscuits are another favourite from my childhood. The secrets to a flavoursome biscuit are to use salted butter and to allow the butter to become quite nut-brown in colour.

Burnt butter biscuits

30 biscuits

250 grams butter
¾ cup sugar
1 egg
few drops almond essence

2 cups pure flour
1 tsp baking powder
70-gram pkt whole blanched almonds

1. Put the butter into a saucepan and place over a moderate heat until the butter has a lovely nut-brown colour to it. Remove the butter from the heat immediately and stand the saucepan on a damp cloth to avoid any further cooking. Scrape any sediment from the base of the saucepan into the butter.
2. When cool, beat in the sugar, egg and almond essence. (The butter will still be liquid.)
3. Sift the flour and baking powder together and stir in.
4. Roll heaped teaspoonfuls of the mixture into balls and place on a greased baking tray. Flatten with your fingers and place an almond onto each biscuit.
5. Bake at 160°C for 15-20 minutes until lightly golden. Cool on a cake rack. Store in an airtight container.

Chinese fortune cookies

14-16 cookies

Make these for children's parties, they'll be a great success.

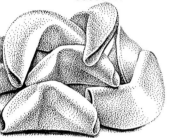

These cookies are heaps of fun. Create your own special fortune messages for friends and serve them after dinner with coffee or for a special party.

½ cup icing sugar
2 egg whites
¼ cup melted butter
½ cup pure flour

1. Sift the icing sugar and set aside.
2. Put the egg whites into a clean bowl and whisk on a low speed just until the egg whites become fluffy.
3. Continue mixing and add the icing sugar and melted butter.
4. Sift the flour and stir into the mixture.
5. Spread about 2 teaspoonfuls of the mixture into an 8 cm circle on a well greased baking tray. Put only three circles onto each tray at any one time.
6. Bake at 180°C for 5-8 minutes until the cookies begin to brown slightly on the edges.
7. Remove from the oven and working quickly lift one cookie off the tray with a palette knife. Place a small piece of paper on which you have written the fortune in the centre of the cookie. Fold the cookie in half to make a semi-circle, only pressing the outer edges together. Then bend the cookie over something sharp-edged like a tea cup to make the shape outlined in the drawing. Cool on a wire rack and keep in an airtight container.

Kourambiethes

40 biscuits

Many traditional Greek cooks lightly brown the butter, as for Burnt Butter Biscuits, and then allow it to re-solidify. This gives these delightful biscuits a completely different flavour.

4 × 70-gram pkt hazelnuts
1 cup icing sugar
2 eggs
200 grams butter
2½ cups pure flour

1½ tsp baking powder
1 tsp cinnamon
about 1 cup extra icing sugar for dusting

1. Toast half the hazelnuts in a 180°C oven for 10 minutes until just beginning to brown. Allow to cool. Process in a food processor with the remaining nuts until finely chopped.
2. Put the icing sugar and eggs into a food processor and process for 2 minutes or until light.
3. Add the softened butter and process for a further 2 minutes or until the mixture is very light and creamy.
4. Sift the flour, baking powder and cinnamon into the food processor bowl and add all the hazelnuts. Process until the mixture is well combined.

5. Roll tablespoonfuls into balls and place on a greased baking tray.

6. Bake at 160°C for 20 minutes or until the cookies are firm and begin to brown lightly.

7. Roll the warm cookies in sifted icing sugar and cool on a cake rack. Store in an airtight container. Dust well with extra sifted icing sugar before serving — these biscuits should be served with a good covering of icing sugar.

Hand/electric beater method

Beat the butter and sugar until light and creamy. Add the eggs and beat well. Using a metal spoon, fold in the ground hazelnuts, sifted flour, baking powder and cinnamon. Continue from step 5.

Oatmeal raisin biscuits

50 biscuits

1 cup sugar
2 eggs
125 grams butter
1 tsp vanilla essence
grated rind 1 lemon

2½ cups pure flour
2½ cups rolled oats
1 cup raisins
icing sugar for decoration

1. Put the sugar and eggs into a food processor and process for 1 minute. Add the butter and process until the mixture becomes creamy.

2. Add the vanilla essence and lemon rind and pulse to mix.

3. Sprinkle the flour, oats and raisins evenly over the creamed mixture and then pulse to mix evenly.

4. Place teaspoonfuls of the mixture on a greased baking tray and allow a little room for spreading.

5. Bake at 180°C for 10-12 minutes until golden.

6. Cool on a cake rack and dust with sifted icing sugar before serving. Store in an airtight container.

Variations:

- Use half raw sugar and half white. The biscuits will not spread as much and will be more cookie-like in texture.
- Use sultanas in place of raisins.
- Use dates, chopped finely, they're delicious in this recipe.

Hand/electric beater method

Beat the butter and sugar together until creamy. Add the eggs, vanilla essence and lemon rind and beat well. Mix in the sifted flour, oats and raisins. Continue from step 4.

Monte Carlos

2 dozen biscuits

These were one of the first packet-type biscuits that I can remember being available. Joined with a sweet raspberry jam and vanilla cream, they were very occasional treats — usually rationed! However the discovery of this recipe has ensured tins full of Monte Carlos.

1 egg
¼ cup sugar
1 tblsp honey
125 grams butter

1 cup self rising flour
1 cup cornflour
¼ cup coconut

Filling
50 grams unsalted butter
¾ cup icing sugar

1 tsp honey
about ½ cup raspberry jam

It's nicer if you sieve the raspberry jam to remove the seeds.

1. Put the egg, sugar and honey into a food processor and process for 2 minutes until light in colour.
2. Add the butter and process a further 2 minutes until the mixture is light and creamy.
3. Sift the flour and cornflour together and sprinkle evenly over the top of the creamed mixture with the coconut. Pulse to mix.
4. Roll small teaspoonfuls into balls and place on a greased baking tray. Flatten firmly with a fork.
5. Bake at 180°C for about 12 minutes or until brown.
6. Transfer to a cake rack to cool. When cold, join together with a little raspberry jam and butter icing. Store in an airtight container.

Butter icing
Beat together butter, icing sugar and 1 teaspoon honey until light and fluffy.

Hand/electric beater method
Beat the butter and sugar together until light and creamy. Add the egg and honey and beat well. Carefully mix in the sifted flour, cornflour and coconut. Continue from step 4.

These large flat biscuits are thin and crisp. They are ideal as a biscuit by themselves or served with poached fruits for a dessert.

250 grams butter
1 cup sugar
2 eggs
2 cups self rising flour

pinch salt
1 tsp ground cinnamon
70-gram pkt pecans

1. Melt the butter over a moderate heat and stir in the sugar. Remove from the heat and allow to cool for 5 minutes.
2. Beat in the eggs.
3. Sift together the flour, salt and cinnamon and stir into the mixture.
4. Place heaped teaspoonfuls onto a greased baking tray and place a pecan in the centre of each. Leave room for the biscuits to spread.
5. Bake at 200°C for 10 minutes until the biscuits have turned a deep brown (not burnt) on the outside.
6. Transfer to a cake rack to cool. Store in an airtight container.

The name says it all really! These biscuits melt in the mouth and are particularly nice if you join them together with a buttery lemon icing.

Melting moments

2 dozen biscuits

275 grams softened unsalted butter
½ cup icing sugar
¼ tsp vanilla essence

1½ cups pure flour
½ cup cornflour
¼ tsp salt

1. Put the butter, icing sugar and vanilla essence into a food processor and process until creamy.
2. Sift together the flour, cornflour and salt and pulse into the creamed mixture. Do not over process.
3. Roll teaspoonfuls into balls and place on a greased baking tray. Press down lightly with a fork.
4. Bake at 160°C for 18-20 minutes until the biscuits are firm and lightly golden, but not brown.
5. Cool on a cake rack. Store in an airtight container.

Variation:
Join two biscuits together with lemon butter icing.

Hand/electric beater method
Beat the butter, sugar and vanilla together until creamy. Mix the sifted flour, cornflour and salt into the creamed mixture with a metal spoon. Continue from step 3.

Cook's Tip:

When decorating the tops of biscuits using a fork, dip the fork into flour to prevent it from sticking to the dough.

Kiss cookies

18-20 cookies

These melt in the mouth and are gently flavoured with mace and lemon zest.

½ cup caster sugar
1 egg
grated rind 1 lemon
125 grams butter
1 cup pure flour

1 cup cornflour
1 tsp baking powder
1 tsp ground mace
½ cup raspberry jam
icing sugar for dusting

1. Put the sugar and egg into a food processor and process for 2 minutes or until lighter in colour.
2. Add the lemon rind and softened butter and process a further 2 minutes or until the mixture is light and creamy.
3. Sift together the flours, baking powder and mace, and sprinkle evenly around the top of the creamed mixture in the processor.
4. Pulse to mix in the flour. Do not over process.
5. Place heaped spoonfuls of mixture onto a greased baking tray. Bake at 180°C for 12-15 minutes until the cookies are firmish to the touch and have begun to brown lightly.
6. Cool on a cake rack. Join two similar-shaped cookies together with raspberry jam and dust with icing sugar. Store in an airtight container.

Hand/electric beater method

Beat the butter and sugar together until light and creamy. Add the egg and lemon rind, and beat well. Mix the sifted flour, cornflour, baking powder and mace and mix into the creamed mixture using a metal spoon. Continue from step 5.

Cook's Tip:

Mace is a very under-used spice. Very popular last century, mace is the blood-red lace-like covering of the nutmeg, which when dried turns rust colour. It can be used whole to flavour hot wine drinks, syrups and sauces, or ground as in this recipe.

Custard dreams

24 biscuits

One of my girlfriend's who helped me proofread this book insisted that the only way to serve these cookies was joined together with jam. Fill them jam-packed with your favourite conserve to follow her mum Dorothy's tradition.

½ cup icing sugar
250 grams unsalted butter
1¾ cups pure flour
pinch salt
½ cup custard powder

1. Put the icing sugar and butter into a food processor and process for 2 minutes until well mixed.
2. Add the flour, salt and custard powder and pulse only until mixed. Do not over process.
3. Roll teaspoonfuls into balls and place on a greased baking tray. Press down with a fork.

Do not overmix in the processor at the Custard Dreams will lose their lovely texture.

Opposite (from top to bottom): Hazelnut (page 59), Wholemeal (page 60), and Orange Biscotti (page 58), and Almond and Angostura Biscotti (page 58).

4. Bake at 180°C for 12–15 minutes until just beginning to turn a pale brown.
5. Cool on a cake rack. Store in an airtight container.

Hand/electric beater method
Beat the butter and sugar to a cream. Sift the flour, salt and custard powder together and work into the creamed mixture with a metal spoon. Continue from step 3.

Afghans

20 biscuits

These are many children's favourite cookies. Crisp with crunchy corn flakes and rich in chocolate, they can also easily be prepared by youngsters.

½ cup firmly packed brown sugar	2 tsp baking powder
1 egg	pinch salt
200 grams unsalted butter	½ cup coconut
1¾ cups flour	2 cups corn flakes
¼ cup cocoa	

1. Put the brown sugar and egg into a food processor and process until the mixture is lighter in colour.
2. Add the softened butter and process a further 2 minutes or until creamy.
3. Sift together the flour, cocoa, baking powder and salt into a clean bowl. Stir through the coconut and corn flakes, and make a well in the centre. Pour in the creamed mixture and mix well with a metal spoon. (I do not complete the entire mix in the food processor as it will crush all the corn flakes.)
4. Spoon large tablespoonfuls of the mixture onto greased trays. Bake at 180°C for 15 minutes.
5. Cool on a cake rack. Store in an airtight container.

Hand/electric beater method
Beat the butter and brown sugar together until creamy. Add the egg and beat well. Mix the sifted flour, cocoa powder, salt, coconut and corn flakes into the creamed mixture with a metal spoon. Continue from step 4.

Rather than ice, decorate these with dusted cocoa or icing sugar.

Cook's Tip:

Even though I call for unsalted butter, a pinch of salt is often added to a recipe to bring out the flavour.

Opposite (from top to bottom): Toll House Biscuits (page 55), Scandinavian Spice Cookies (page 56), Kourambiethes (page 44), Butter Biscuits (page 41), Kiss Cookies (page 48).

Iced vo vo biscuits

30 biscuits

This is a great biscuit for children to make as they will love decorating them to look like the ones in the packets. They're far more tasty and more economical.

2 cups pure flour
125 grams butter
½ cup caster sugar
2 eggs

milk
about ½ cup raspberry jam
coconut

Marshmallow topping
200-gram pkt pink marshmallows

1.   Put the flour into a food processor. Add the butter and process until the mixture resembles fine crumbs.
2.   Pulse in the sugar.
3.   Beat the eggs lightly, add to the dry ingredients and pulse to form a stiff dough. You may need to add 1 or 2 tablespoons of milk.
4.   Roll the dough out on a floured board to 2–3 mm thickness.
5.   Cut into round or rectangular biscuits. The size depends on you, but I cut them out to shapes of about 3 cm × 5 cm.
6.   Place on a greased tray and bake at 180°C for 15-20 minutes or until the biscuits are crisp and golden.
7.   Cool on a cake rack. When cold, pipe a line of jam down the centre. Pipe a line of the marshmallow topping on either side and turn the biscuits over and press into coconut. Store in an airtight container.

Marshmallow topping
Melt all the pink marshmallows in the microwave for about 15-20 seconds (only until melted). Pour into a piping bag fitted with a narrow nozzle.

By hand
Sift the flour into a bowl. Rub in the butter until the mixture resembles fine crumbs. Mix in the sugar. Beat the eggs and mix into the dry ingredients. Add a tablespoon or two of milk if necessary to form a soft dough. Continue from step 4.

Honey biscuits

5 dozen biscuits

The traditional Greek name for these cookies is Melomakarona. They are truly wonderful.

½ cup pure flour
2¾ cups self rising flour
1 tsp mixed spice
125 grams butter
grated rind 1 orange or lemon

¾ cup light olive oil
½ cup fresh orange juice
1 tblsp brandy
½ cup finely chopped walnuts

Syrup
½ cup liquid honey
¼ cup water
1 tblsp ground cinnamon

1. Put the flours and mixed spice together into a food processor and pulse to mix.
2. Add the butter and process until the mixture resembles crumbs.
3. Mix together the orange rind, olive oil, orange juice and brandy. Pour into the bowl and pulse to form a soft dough. Add a little extra flour if too soft.
4. Take dessertspoonfuls of the mixture and roll into balls the shape of an egg. Place on a greased baking tray. Flatten slightly with your fingers.
5. Bake at 190°C for 15 minutes or until golden.
6. Dip the warm biscuits into the syrup and then top with the chopped walnuts. Allow to cool on the cake rack. Store in an airtight container.

Syrup
Mix together the honey, water and cinnamon and simmer for 3-5 minutes.

By hand
Sift the flours and mixed spice into a bowl. Rub in the butter until the mixture resembles fine crumbs. Make a well in the centre. Mix the remaining ingredients together and pour in. Mix with a knife to form a soft dough. Continue from step 4.

Why not try scented rose geranium leaves in the syrup in place of cinnamon. Allow 2–3 leaves to infuse and then remove.

Spooky-faced cookies

Makes 36 cookies

This recipe appeared in my Halloween special for *Next* magazine in 1992. They were one of the ideas for a Halloween party, prepared for me by Ann Boardman who, with three children, is an expert in party foods for youngsters. More so than me! We also had Lanterns, which was chocolate cake mixture cooked in oranges, a white chocolate mousse called a Ghost Cake, and Bat's Blood Soda, made from strawberries and orange juice with soda. All the right ingredients for a children's Halloween party.

1 egg
125 grams butter
1 cup brown sugar
1 tblsp peanut butter
½ cup blanched peanuts

1 tblsp water
¾ cup pure flour
½ tsp baking soda
1½ cups rolled oats

Butter icing

50 grams butter
1½ cups icing sugar

½ tsp vanilla essence
3–4 tsp warm water

To decorate

Lifesavers, Pebbles, chocolate bits, liquorice assortments, flaked almonds, etc. Almost any lollies will do.

1. Put the egg, butter, sugar, peanut butter, peanuts and water into a food processor and process until the peanuts are finely chopped and the ingredients well mixed.
2. Add the flour, baking soda and rolled oats and pulse only until the flour is well combined. Do not over process.
3. Place heaped teaspoonfuls of the mixture onto a greased baking tray. With a wet fork press the cookies out to a 4-5 cm diameter.
4. Bake at 180°C for about 12 minutes until the cookies have browned lightly and become firm. Transfer to a cake rack to cool.
5. Spread each cookie with icing. Using the lollies, decorate each cookie with a different face. Store in an airtight container.

Icing

Beat the butter, icing sugar and vanilla essence until light and creamy. If too thick add a little water to make a spreadable consistency.

Cook's Tip:

Buy small quantities of lollies from the bulk candy bin department at the supermarket.

The combination of orange and chocolate in a rich buttery biscuit will always be a winner.

1 cup icing sugar
1 egg
grated rind of 2 oranges
300 grams unsalted butter

½ cup cocoa
2½ cups pure flour
100 grams cooking chocolate
1 tsp Kremelta

Jaffa butter biscuits

40 biscuits

1. Put the icing sugar, egg and orange rind into a food processor and process for 2 minutes.
2. Add the softened butter and process a further 2 minutes until the mixture is light and fluffy.
3. Sift together the cocoa and flour and sprinkle evenly over the top of the creamed mixture. Pulse to mix. Do not over process.
4. Put the mixture into a piping bag fitted with a large star nozzle and pipe medium-sized rosettes onto a greased baking tray.
5. Bake at 180°C for 12-15 minutes. Cool on a cake rack.
6. Melt the chocolate and the Kremelta in a bowl over hot water or in a microwave. Spread a little of the melted chocolate on the base of each cookie and allow to set. Alternatively pipe thin ribbons of chocolate over the top of each cookie. Store in an airtight container.

Hand/electric beater method
Beat the butter and icing sugar until light and creamy. Add the egg and orange rind and beat well. Mix in the sifted cocoa and flour with a metal spoon. Continue from step 4.

These were another all-time favourite in our house when I was growing up. I think that was because they are so easy to make.

2 cups self rising flour
125 grams butter
½ cup sugar
1 cup mixed dried fruit

¼ cup milk
1 egg
grated rind 2 lemons

Rock cakes

24 cakes

1. Sift the flour into a bowl.
2. Cut in the butter until the mixture resembles fine crumbs. Stir through the sugar and mixed dried fruit and make a well in the centre.
3. Mix together the milk, egg and lemon rind and pour into the well. Mix with a knife to make a soft dough.
4. Place tablespoonfuls of the mixture onto a greased baking tray.
5. Bake at 200°C for 12-15 minutes or until the cakes are lightly browned.
6. Cool on a cake rack. Store in an airtight container.

Nan Berinji

40 biscuits

These Persian rice cookies are heavily scented with cardamom, my favourite spice. The rice flour gives them their traditional short grainy texture.

500 grams unsalted butter
1 cup icing sugar
1 tblsp ground cardamom
2 tblsp rosewater

1 egg
4 cups rice flour
1 tsp baking powder

1. Put the butter, icing sugar, ground cardamom, rosewater and egg into a food processor and process until well combined.
2. Sift the rice flour and baking powder together and sprinkle evenly over the top of the creamed mixture. Pulse to mix. Do not over process.
3. Roll teaspoonfuls of the mixture into balls and place on a greased baking tray. Press down with a fork.
4. Bake at 180°C for 20 minutes until the cookies have begun to brown lightly.
5. Cool on a cake rack. Store in an airtight container.

Hand/electric beater method

Beat the butter and sugar together until light and creamy. Add the egg and rosewater and beat well. Mix the sifted rice flour, baking powder and cardamom into the creamed mixture with a metal spoon. Continue from step 3.

Cook's Tip:

Rosewater is made by distilling fragrant rose petals. The rosewater available in supermarkets is a poor second to the real thing, which you can buy in specialty shops. Crabtree & Evelyn has an excellent variety.

Bobby's peanut biscuits

30 biscuits

Bobby was my godmother, a very kind woman who would never let a birthday or Christmas go by without a special gift. These were her favourite biscuits, and I share her recipe with you.

1 cup caster sugar
1 egg
125 grams butter
1 cup self rising flour

½ cup chopped peanuts
1 cup rolled oats
1 cup corn flakes

1. Put the sugar and egg into a food processor and process for 2 minutes until much lighter in colour.
2. Add the softened butter and process a further 2 minutes until well combined.
3. Sprinkle the flour evenly over the top of the creamed mixture. On top of the flour put the peanuts, then the rolled oats and lastly the corn flakes.
4. Pulse only until the ingredients have mixed.
5. Place tablespoonfuls of the mixture onto a greased baking tray.
6. Bake at 180°C for 15 minutes or until the biscuits have browned.
7. Cool on a cake rack. Store in an airtight container.

Hand/electric beater method

Beat the butter and sugar together until light and creamy. Add the egg and beat well. Mix in the sifted flour with the rolled oats, corn flakes and chopped peanuts. Continue from step 5.

Cook's Tip:

By layering the ingredients in the food processor, you can mix in ingredients that need delicate handling. Always put the delicate ingredients, which can be crushed, last.

Toll house biscuits

30 biscuits

Toll House Biscuits are reputed to be the world's first chocolate chip cookies and naturally they come from America. They were created by a Mrs Ruth Wakefield who ran the Toll House restaurant in Massachussets, who cut up pieces of chocolate from a large bar and added it to a basic biscuit recipe. Well, that's the legend I know and love anyway.

¾ cup brown sugar
¾ cup caster sugar
2 eggs
175 grams unsalted butter

2¼ cups pure flour
1 tsp baking powder
pinch salt
2 cups chocolate chips

1. Put the brown sugar, caster sugar and eggs into a food processor and process for 2 minutes until lighter in colour and well mixed.
2. Add the softened butter and process a further 2 minutes until the mixture is light and creamy.
3. Sift together the flour, baking powder and salt and sprinkle evenly over the top of the creamed mixture. Sprinkle the chocolate chips on top of the flour.
4. Pulse to mix. Do not over process as the chocolate chips will be too finely chopped.
5. Place heaped tablespoonfuls of mixture onto a greased baking tray, leaving room for the cookies to spread.
6. Bake at 180°C for 20 minutes or until the biscuits are beginning to brown lightly and are firm to the touch.
7. Transfer to a cake rack to cool. Store in an airtight container.

Hand/electric beater method

Beat the butter, brown and caster sugar together until light and creamy. Add the eggs and beat well. Fold in the sifted flour and baking powder with the chocolate chips using a metal spoon. Continue from step 5.

Cook's Tip:

Buy chocolate chips that look like little round chips, not drops. Do not use chocolate hail.

Scandinavian spice cookies

40 biscuits

Traditionally these cookies are prepared in hand-carved wooden biscuit moulds. To make it easier, I have prepared them here another way.

250 grams unsalted butter
1 cup caster sugar
¼ cup golden syrup
1 tblsp liquid honey
70-gram pkt flaked almonds
½ tsp cinnamon

2 tsp ground cardamom
1 tsp ground ginger
1 tsp baking soda
1 tblsp water
3 cups pure flour

Cardamom hails from India but is the flavour most recognised in Scandinavian baking. Its warm, pungent and spicy fragrance is wonderful in these cookies.

1. Put the butter, caster sugar, golden syrup, honey, almonds, cinnamon, cardamom and ginger into a saucepan and stir gently over a moderate heat until the butter has melted. Bring to the boil and then remove from the heat.
2. Dissolve the baking soda in the water and stir into the butter mixture. Leave to cool.
3. Sift the flour into a large bowl and make a well in the centre.
4. Pour in the butter mixture and, using a wooden spoon, mix to a stiff dough. Turn out onto a floured board and knead lightly.
5. Divide the mixture in half and roll each half into a log about 4–5 cm in diameter. Wrap each log in plastic wrap and refrigerate for 4 hours or until very firm.
6. Cut the logs into 0.5 cm slices and place on a greased baking tray.
7. Bake at 180°C for 12-15 minutes until deep golden brown, but not burnt.
8. Transfer to a cake rack to cool. Store in an airtight container.

Opposite (clockwise from left): Oatcakes (page 64), Water Crackers (page 65), Cream Crackers (page 64), Sesame Crackers (page 66).

Following page (from back to front): Scotch Shortbread (page 70), Brown Sugar Shortbread (page 69), Basic Shortbread with lavender flowers (page 68).

BISCOTTI

These tempting treats have become one of the fashions of the 1990s, and are an ideal nibble for almost any time of the day.

If you have not come across them before, biscotti means twice cooked and that's exactly what you do. They're extremely crunchy, jam packed with nuts, gently spiced, and often contain a little vino for good flavour. Tradition has it that these molar-testing biscuits originated in Tuscany in Northern Italy. Until recently in New Zealand they could only be bought from delicatessens, imported from their country of origin.

Biscotti should be served dunked in wine, red or a sweet white, or in freshly brewed coffee. You can eat them without dunking but beware!

The best results are achieved by using a hand-held beater. While they may take a little time to prepare, biscotti keep for a long time and are well worth the effort. Almond and Angostura Biscotti are my favourites.

Preceding page (from back to front): Double Chocolate Shortbread (page 70), Passionfruit Shortbread (page 71), Almond Shortbread (page 72).

Opposite: American Strawberry Shortcake (page 78).

Almond and angostura biscotti

48 biscotti

Angostura Bitters' trademark is their unique bottle. Bitters are made from a distillation of herbs, barks, roots and plants. They are distinctly bitter or bittersweet and are often forgotten when cooking. They enhance any fruit salad — try it, just a few drops will do.

Cook's Tip:

It is often best to flour as well as grease baking trays to ensure that baked goods can be removed easily after cooking.

Crisp golden almonds, flavoured with Angostura Bitters, make a super combination in this biscotti recipe.

70-gram pkt whole unblanched almonds
125 grams unsalted butter
¾ cup sugar
2 eggs
1 tblsp Angostura Bitters
2 cups pure flour
¼ tsp salt
1½ tsp baking powder

1. Toast the almonds in a 180°C oven for about 10 minutes until they smell nutty. Watch them carefully as they will burn quickly.
2. Cool and chop them into chunky pieces.
3. Beat the butter and sugar to a cream. Beat in the eggs one at a time, beating well until the mixture is smooth.
4. Beat in the Angostura Bitters.
5. Sift together the flour, salt and baking powder.
6. Add the sifted ingredients and almonds to the creamed mixture and stir only until combined.
7. On a lightly floured board make sausage-like rolls of dough about 3 cm in diameter and the length of the baking tray. Place them on a greased baking tray about 5 cm apart.
8. Bake at 160°C for 25 minutes or until they are set and lightly browned on top.
9. Cool the rolls on a cake rack for 10 minutes then slice them diagonally into 1 cm slices.
10. Lay the slices back on the tray and return them to the oven for a further 5 minutes. Turn them over and cook a further 5 minutes. They should be slightly toasted in colour but not too brown. Cool on a cake rack and keep in an airtight container.

Variations:

If you don't have Angostura Bitters, use a liqueur that will accompany almonds. Try Amaretto, Grand Marnier or Cointreau.

Orange biscotti

48 biscotti

1½ cups whole unblanched almonds
2½ cups pure flour
½ tsp baking powder
1 tsp baking soda
¼ tsp salt
1 cup sugar
3 eggs
few drops almond essence
1 tsp orange blossom water
1 tblsp grated orange rind
½ cup chopped dried apples (optional)

1. Toast the almonds in a 180°C oven for about 10 minutes until they begin to smell nutty and are just beginning to show signs of colouring.
2. Sift together the flour, baking powder, baking soda, salt and sugar.
3. Whisk together the eggs, almond essence, orange blossom water and orange rind until the mixture becomes light.

4. Add the egg mixture to the dry ingredients, stirring until a soft dough is formed. Stir in the almonds and apples.

5. Turn the dough out onto a floured board and knead it lightly for about 3 minutes.

6. Shape the dough into sausage-like rolls about 3 cm in diameter and the length of the baking tray, and flatten them slightly. Place on a greased tray about 5 cm apart.

7. Bake the logs at 160°C for 30 minutes until they feel set to the touch. Allow them to cool for 10 minutes on the baking tray.

8. Cut the rolls on the diagonal into 0.5-1 cm thick slices. Place on a tray and return these to the oven for a further 5-7 minutes each side. They should be a light toasted colour. Cool on a cake rack and store in airtight containers.

Cook's Tip:

When blending flour into eggs, use a holed spoon. It will help mix the ingredients together.

Hazelnut biscotti

40 biscotti

Hazelnuts are my favourite nut. They add flavour to both savoury and sweet dishes. I make a hazelnut butter (like peanut), which is very decadent but ever-so yummy. Enjoy these Hazelnut Biscotti with liqueur coffees — try Frangelico mixed with Cointreau — absolutely wonderful!

3 × 70-gram pkts hazelnuts   *125 grams unsalted butter*
2½ cups pure flour   *1 cup sugar*
1 tsp baking powder   *3 eggs*
½ tsp baking soda   *1 tsp freshly grated lemon rind*
½ tsp salt   *1½ tsp vanilla essence*

1. Toast the hazelnuts in a 180°C oven for about 12-15 minutes until the hazelnuts begin to brown and are lightly toasted. Skin and chop roughly.

2. Sift together the flour, baking powder, baking soda and salt.

3. Beat the butter and sugar together until the mixture is light and fluffy. Add the eggs one at a time, beating well after each addition.

4. Beat in the lemon rind and vanilla essence.

5. Stir in the flour and hazelnuts.

6. Turn out onto a lightly floured board and knead for about 1 minute. Shape into sausage-like rolls about 3 cm in diameter and the length of your baking tray. Flatten the logs a little.

7. Bake at 160°C for 30 minutes then allow the logs to cool on the tray for 10 minutes.

8. Cut the logs on the diagonal into 0.5-1 cm pieces. Place the biscotti on the tray and return to the oven for 5 minutes. Turn them over and cook a further 5 minutes. They should be a light toasted colour. Cool on a cake rack and store in airtight containers.

Cook's Tip:

Skin hazelnuts by taking a handful of cooled nuts and rubbing your hands together over a sink, allowing the skins to fall away freely. Or put the hazelnuts into a clean teatowel and rub together.

Wholemeal biscotti

32 biscotti

1 cup pecans or walnuts (or a mix of both)
1½ cups pure flour
1 cup sugar
1 tsp baking soda
¼ tsp salt
½ tsp cinnamon
1 cup wholemeal flour
3 eggs
¼ cup port

1. Toast the pecans or walnuts in a 180°C oven for 10–12 minutes until lightly toasted. Chop roughly.
2. In a large bowl sift together the pure flour, sugar, baking soda, salt and cinnamon. Stir in the wholemeal flour.
3. Beat the eggs until light then add the port. Gradually blend the eggs and port into the flour to form a smooth dough. Stir in the toasted nuts.
4. Turn the dough onto a lightly floured board and knead for 1 minute. Shape into sausage-like rolls about 3 cm in diameter and as long as the baking tray. Place on a greased tray and flatten slightly.
5. Bake at 160°C for 30 minutes. Allow the rolls to cool on the tray for 10 minutes.
6. Cut the rolls diagonally into 0.5-1 cm wide slices. Place on the tray and return to the oven for 5 minutes. Turn over and cook for a further 5 minutes. They should become a light toasted colour. Transfer to a cake rack to cool before storing in an airtight container.

Variation:
Add dried fruits, such as 1 cup chopped dried apple or papaya.

Cook's Tip:

Nuts contain high amounts of oil and as a result will go rancid if left in warm places. It is best to keep nuts in the freezer and use as required.

Chocolate and almond biscotti

36 biscotti

Try these chocolate morsels dipped in your favourite liqueur or the traditional Italian accompaniment, Grappa.

2 × 70-gram pkt blanched almonds
2 cups pure flour
¾ cup caster sugar
pinch salt
1 tsp baking soda
½ tsp baking powder
½ cup chocolate chips
2 eggs
1 egg white

1. Toast the almonds in a 180°C oven for 15 minutes or until golden brown. Allow the nuts to cool.
2. Put one-third of the nuts into a food processor and process until finely milled.
3. In a bowl sift the flour, sugar, salt, baking soda and baking powder. Stir through the ground almonds and the chocolate chips.
4. Beat the whole eggs together lightly.
5. Make a well in the centre and add the beaten eggs and mix with a wooden spoon to make a thick dough.
6. Turn out onto a lightly floured board and knead for 1-2 minutes.
7. Divide the dough into 3 pieces and roll each piece out into a sausage

shape about 2 cm in diameter and the length of your baking tray. Place each roll on a greased baking tray.

8. Brush the rolls with lightly beaten egg white.

9. Bake at 180°C for 20 minutes. Remove and allow to cool for 10 minutes.

10. Cut the rolls into 1 cm slices on the diagonal and place the pieces back on the baking tray. Return to a 140°C oven for a further 20 minutes, turning the biscotti over after 10 minutes. Cool on a cake rack. Store in an airtight container.

Cook's Tip:

Use a serrated-edge knife when cutting biscotti into thin slices; the serrated knife will cut through the nuts more evenly.

Lemon hazelnut bread

24 slices

Not quite a biscotti, this is made like a loaf and then cut into thin slices.

3 egg whites
pinch of cream of tartar
½ cup caster sugar
¾ cup pure flour
2 × 70-gram pkt hazelnuts (lightly toasted)
grated rind 1 lemon

1. In a clean bowl beat the egg whites and cream of tartar with a hand-held beater or wire whisk until they are stiff but not dry.

2. Gradually beat in the sugar. The sugar should all be dissolved and the mixture thick and meringue-like.

3. Sift the flour and fold into the meringue mixture with the chopped hazelnuts and grated lemon rind.

4. Transfer the mixture to a well greased, floured and paper-lined 7 cm × 22 cm loaf tin.

5. Bake at 150°C for 30-40 minutes or until firm to the touch.

6. Allow to cool in the tin before turning out. Wrap in foil and store for two days. Using a serrated-edge knife, cut the bread into wafer-thin slices and place on a baking tray.

7. Bake at 120°C for 30 minutes or until the slices are dry and lightly golden. Store in an airtight container.

Cook's Tip:

Egg whites will whip better if you add a pinch of cream of tartar. Beat slowly at first, then increase speed.

Pistachio and almond bread

24 slices

If you can, use only pistachio nuts that have open shells. They're easier to shell and, more importantly, closed shell nuts were immature when picked.

These feather-light slices make just the right accompaniment to coffee at the end of a rich meal.

4 egg whites
pinch cream of tartar
½ cup caster sugar
few drops almond essence

½ cup plus 2 tblsp pure flour
1 cup combined shelled pistachio nuts
*   and flaked almonds*

1. Put the egg whites into a clean bowl and beat slowly with a whisk or a hand-held beater until the egg whites become frothy. Add the cream of tartar and continue beating until the egg whites are stiff but not dry.
2. Add the caster sugar and beat until the sugar has dissolved and the meringue is thick. Beat in the almond essence.
3. Sift the flour and fold into the egg whites with the nuts.
4. Turn the mixture into a greased and paper lined 7 cm × 22 cm loaf tin.
5. Bake at 180°C for 45 minutes until the loaf is firm. Turn out onto a cake rack to cool.
6. When cold, cut into thin slices and place on a tray. Bake at 140°C for 15 minutes, until the slices are lightly golden. Turn and do the other side for approximately 5 minutes. Be careful as they brown and burn quickly. Cool on a cake rack. Store in an airtight container. They will keep for several weeks.

Cook's Tip:

Pistachio nuts are wonderful in taste and colour, but so time consuming to shell. Try to find them already shelled. They will be much more expensive, but you will keep your cool (I lost mine!).

SAVOURY BISCUITS

Crunchy, wafer-thin, seasoned savoury biscuits are incredibly simple to make. Armed with your food processor you will soon discover that homemade water crackers are far more tasty than those purchased in your supermarket. They have more body for eating with tasty cheeses and rich patés, and you are able to add your own special touches in the way of spices and herbs.

Oatcakes

30 oatcakes

Oatcakes are deliciously nutty and best served with a tasty cheddar and good pickle. If you are entertaining, they make a super accompaniment to a coarse pork or game paté.

4 cups fine oatmeal or oat flakes
1 tsp baking powder
¼ tsp salt
¼ cup melted butter
1¼ cups boiling water

Don't forget the salt. Without it savoury biscuits will be tasteless and you will never enjoy them.

1. Put the oatmeal, baking powder and salt into a food processor and pulse to mix.
2. With the motor running, pour the melted butter and water down the feed tube as fast as the oats can absorb it.
3. Turn out onto a board dusted with a little oatmeal and knead lightly. Roll out as thin as possible; if the edges keep breaking, pinch them together.
4. Cut into 8 cm rounds. Use a slide to transfer to a greased baking tray as the oatcakes are very delicate.
5. Bake at 190°C for 15-20 minutes or until the oatcakes are a pale fawn shade.
6. Cool on a cake rack and store in an airtight container.

Cream crackers

60 crackers

So named because they are made with sour cream.

1 cup pure flour
¼ tsp salt
½ cup oat bran
2 tsp sugar
¼ tsp baking soda
75 grams butter
½ cup sour cream

1. Put the flour, salt, oat bran, sugar and baking soda into a food processor and pulse to sift.
2. Add the butter and process until the mixture resembles fine crumbs.
3. Add the sour cream and process until the mixture forms a soft dough. Depending on the flour, you may need to add a teaspoon or so of water.
4. Turn the dough out onto a floured board and knead for 10 minutes. Cover the dough with a clean teatowel and rest 10 minutes.
5. Roll the dough out to about 2-3 mm thickness. Cut into 5 cm rounds and place on a greased baking tray. Prick the crackers with a fork all over.
6. Bake at 200°C for 8–10 minutes until firm. Cool on a cake rack. Keep in an airtight container.

Cook's Tip:

These biscuits will keep well frozen. Refresh by placing in a warm oven for a few minutes once defrosted.

Variations:
- Use wholemeal flour in place of oat bran.
- Brush the crackers with a little milk and sprinkle with sesame seeds or poppy seeds.
- Omit the bran and add ½ cup white flour for plain crackers.

Opposite: Jewel Cake (page 88).

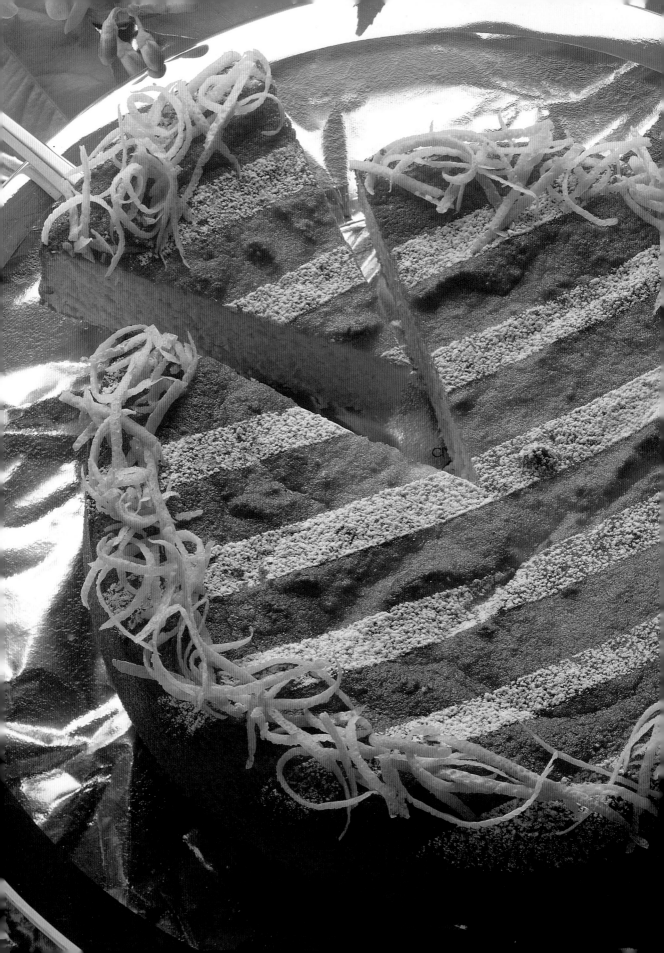

Vary the recipe by using sesame seeds in place of poppy seeds.

3½ cups pure flour
large pinch salt
40-gram pkt poppy seeds
75 grams butter
1 cup milk

1. Put the flour, salt and poppy seeds into a food processor and pulse to sift.
2. Add the butter and process until the mixture looks like crumbs.
3. With the motor running, pour the liquid down the feed tube until all the milk has been absorbed. Process the dough for a full minute.
4. Turn the dough out onto a floured board and bring together. Cover with plastic wrap and leave to rest for 10 minutes.
5. Roll the dough out on a lightly floured surface as thinly as possible. Cut into circles of your preferred size. Place on a greased baking tray and prick thoroughly with a fork all over.
6. Bake at 190°C for 10-12 minutes until the biscuits are light golden.
7. Cool the biscuits on a cake rack. Store in an airtight container

Water crackers

48 8 cm round biscuits

Cook's Tip:

You can add dried herbs to this recipe to enhance the flavour of the crackers if you like. About ½ tsp of your favourite should be enough. Try sweet basil or dill.

These are my regular stand-by for when guests call in unexpectedly. Make up a batch and keep them in the freezer; refresh quickly in a warm oven. Serve as they are, as an accompaniment to pesto, paté or guacamole, or top them with slices of smoked salmon and sour cream.

equal quantities by weight of flour, butter and tasty cheddar cheese

Toppings
sesame seeds, poppy seeds, finely chopped nuts of your choice

1. Put the flour into a food processor and pulse to sift.
2. Grate the butter and cheese into the flour. Process until the mixture forms a stiff ball of dough.
3. Turn out onto a lightly floured board and roll the dough out to 0.5–1 cm thickness. Cut into rounds or preferred shapes. Place on an ungreased baking tray and top with one of the selected toppings.
4. Bake at 200°C for 12-15 minutes or until golden and crisp.
5. Cool on a cake rack. Store in an airtight container or freeze when cold.

Variations:
- Use ½ wholemeal and ½ plain flour.
- Add 25 grams blue cheese to the recipe.

Cheese sables

100 grams of each ingredient will give you approximately 24 sables

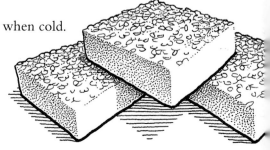

Opposite: John's Turkish Orange Cake (page 92).

Sesame crackers

36 crackers

These crackers are an ideal muncher for young children. Low in fat, topped with a piece of cheese they are great for after school.

1 cup pure flour
1 cup wholemeal flour
1 tsp salt
¼ tsp baking soda

2 tblsp sesame seeds
1 tblsp butter
¼ cup plain unsweetened yoghurt
½ cup chilled water

1. Put the flours, salt and baking soda into a food processor.
2. Toast the sesame seeds in the butter until lightly golden and add to the flour.
3. Mix the yoghurt and water together and with the motor running pour the liquid down the feed tube. Process until the mixture forms a soft ball of dough.
4. Turn out onto a lightly floured board and knead lightly. Cover with a clean towel and stand 10 minutes.
5. Roll the dough out very thinly. Cut into preferred shapes and place on a greased tray. Prick the crackers all over with a fork.
6. Bake at 180°C for 10 minutes or until lightly golden.
7. Cool on a cake rack. Store in an airtight container.

Variations:
- Use poppy, caraway or celery seeds.
- Use rye flour in place of wholemeal.

SHORTBREAD

Melting with good taste, shortbread is my favourite year-round biscuit. I have an aunt (Phyl), who makes the best shortbread going, but like so many great family cooks, her recipe is a guarded secret that I'm told is never the same twice!

The crimped edge that we associate with traditional Scottish shortbread was meant to signify the sun's rays. If you have moulds, use them — the finished product looks wonderful.

Try the nutty wholemeal version, it is a real winner.

Cook's Tip:

To use wooden moulds, rub the moulds with cornflour, take a small piece of dough and place it in the centre of the mould. Using a rolling pin, roll the dough into the mould until the mould is full and the shortbread smooth and even on top. Trim the edges and then turn out onto the tray. Use this method for small or large moulds.

Basic shortbread

It was much easier to write this recipe in the days of imperial measures. You need 4 oz icing sugar, 8 oz good butter, 12 oz flour and a pinch of salt. The recipe was easy to increase or decrease depending on how much shortbread was required. It was one of the first recipes I collected and was taught to me by a godmother, Aunt Jean. Now in her 80s, Aunt Jean still has this on hand when I go home.

I try to write all my recipes as simply as possible, generally using cup measurements. But on this occasion I have done a straight conversion in measurements to ensure the same proportions and traditional taste.

For such a simple and popular biscuit, there is more controversy on how to make shortbread than on any other baked goods!

The ingredients: butter, salted or unsalted, never margarine (sorry margarine lovers, the taste is not the same). I prefer the salted butter but try unsalted. Sugar — icing, caster or ordinary white! They will all give you a different texture. I prefer caster sugar shortbread as it has a more crunchy texture.

The method is also a good point of discussion, depending on which relative taught you how to make shortbread. Some people cream the butter and sugar until light and creamy, others work the butter and sugar together by hand and then work in the flour. Different methods give a different texture, so experiment. When I am making shortbread in a hurry I always use the food processor — it saves so much time and effort.

The next point of contention with shortbread is the temperature that you cook it at. (And I said it was a simple thing!) Some people prefer to cook it slowly and for a long time, others at a higher temperature for a shorter time. There is nothing worse than a party of dedicated shortbread makers all trying to insist that their way is best! And it's even worse if there is some Scottish heritage floating around (ohoo noo!).

Anyway, here's the version my godmother Jean taught me when I was about 10, and even though I use the processor these days the taste is still pretty much the same now as it was back then.

250 grams butter
125 grams sugar (icing or caster)
350 grams pure flour
pinch salt

1. Beat the butter and sugar together until light and creamy in colour. It should be pale and the sugar, if using caster, dissolved.
2. Sift the flour and salt together three times and work this carefully into the butter.
3. Place the mixture into the fridge for about 1 hour until it is firm enough to handle. Turn out onto a floured board and knead lightly (see floral variations).
4. Roll the dough out to a 1 cm thickness and cut into circles or bar

shapes. Place on a tray and mark the tops with a fork.

5. Bake at 160°C for 25–30 minutes or until firm but golden and not brown.

6. Cool on a wire rack and store in an airtight container. Shortbread tastes best when it has had time to allow the flavours to blend, about 7 days.

Food processor method

Soften the butter. Put the butter and sugar into a food processor and process for 2 minutes until light. Add the flour and salt and pulse until incorporated.

Variations:

* Roll the dough out as above and cut into 16–20 cm circles. Transfer to a greased tray and mark into wedges with a sharp knife. Pinch the edges into a decorative pattern. Bake as above but allow an extra 10 minutes.
* **Lavender Shortbread**. Add ¼ cup lavender flowers to the shortbread mix when kneading lightly.
* **Rose Shortbread**. Add ½ cup scented rose petals to the shortbread mix when kneading lightly. If wished, add a drop of red food colouring as well.

Cook's Tip:

To cut time, roll the prepared dough into 3 cm sausage-shaped rounds. Refrigerate for 1 hour. Cut into 1 cm rounds and place on the baking tray. The mixture can also be frozen at this point. What I do is cut the rounds, re-assemble the log, roll it in baking paper, place in an airtight bag, and freeze. That way you can break off and bake as many biscuits as you want at any one time.

½ cup firmly packed soft brown sugar
250 grams butter
1¾ cups pure flour
½ cup cornflour
½ tsp salt

1. Put the brown sugar and butter into a food processor and process until light and creamy.
2. Sift the flour, cornflour and salt together and add to the food processor.
3. Pulse the ingredients together until just combined.
4. Turn the mixture out onto a floured board and knead together.
5. Roll the dough out to 1–1.5 cm thickness and cut into rounds. Place on a greased baking tray.
6. Bake at 160°C for 35–40 minutes until firm to the touch.
7. Allow to cool on the tray for 10 minutes before transferring to a cake rack to cool. Store in an airtight container.

Brown sugar shortbread

24 pieces

Don't forget the salt in shortbread — it needs at least a good pinch to bring out the buttery flavour.

Scotch shortbread

30-35 pieces

Sprinkle a little caster sugar onto the shortbread before cooking if wished.

200 grams butter
½ cup caster sugar
2 cups pure flour
¼ cup rice flour
¼ tsp salt

1. Beat the butter and sugar together until light and creamy.
2. Sift the flour, rice flour and salt together and work into the creamed mixture.
3. Press the mixture into a greased, floured and lined 20 cm × 30 cm slice tin.
4. Mark into squares or bars and mark each piece three times with a fork.
5. Bake at 160°C for 50-60 minutes.
6. Cool in the tin for 30 minutes before turning out and cutting into pieces using the lines already marked on the shortbread. Cool on a cake rack. Store in an airtight container.

Food processor method

Soften the butter. Put the butter and sugar into a processor and process until light — about 2 minutes. Add the rice flour, flour and salt and pulse until well mixed.

Cook's Tip:

Rice flour is a fine powdery flour made from regular white rice. It gives this shortbread its characteristic texture and flavour. If you do not have it, try cornflour. While it will not give you the same texture, it will give another flavour variation.

Double chocolate shortbread

35 pieces

Definitely one for the chocoholics out there!

250 grams butter
¾ cup caster sugar
2¼ cups pure flour
¼ cup cocoa
1 tsp salt
½ cup chocolate chips

1. Put the butter and sugar into a food processor and process until smooth and creamy.
2. Sift the flour, cocoa and salt together and add to the food processor. Pulse to mix.
3. Add the chocolate chips and pulse until the chips are incorporated.
4. Turn the mixture onto a floured board and bring together. Refrigerate for 1 hour if you have time.
5. Roll the dough out to 1 cm thickness and cut into 35 equal-shape bars. Place on a greased baking tray.

6. Bake at 160°C for 30 minutes.

7. Cool on the tray for 10 minutes before transferring to a cake rack. Store in an airtight container when cold.

Cook's Tip:

Butter and sugar beaten together in the food processor will not be as light and creamy as that beaten by beaters. However, it is doubly quick and the end product is still good.

Passionfruit shortbread

24 pieces

Delicately flavoured, these shortbread are nice with a cup of herbal tea.

¼ cup fresh passionfruit pulp
150 grams unsalted butter
½ cup icing sugar

¼ cup cornflour
1½ cups flour
pinch salt

1. Sieve the passionfruit pulp to remove the seeds. You need about 2 tablespoons of pulp.

2. Beat the butter and icing sugar together until light and creamy. Beat in the passionfruit pulp mixture.

3. Sift the cornflour, flour and salt together and work into the dry ingredients.

4. Turn out onto a floured board and bring together.

5. Roll out to 1 cm thickness. Cut into shapes or rounds. Place on a greased baking tray and mark with a fork.

6. Bake at 160°C for 20 minutes or until lightly golden.

7. Leave on the tray for 10 minutes before transferring to a cake rack to cool. Store in an airtight container.

Cook's Tip:

Freeze passionfruit pulp when it is in season for use later in the year. Scoop the pulp from the fruit and distribute evenly in ice cube containers. Freeze. When frozen, transfer the cubes to a bag and tie with a twisty-tie. Use cubes as required.

Almond shortbread

20 pieces

Try lemon for a tangier shortbread.

This shortbread is very crunchy and ideal for dunking in tea or coffee. Don't leave it too long though — you'll end up with a soggy biscuit!

1 cup pure flour
1 cup caster sugar
1 cup whole unblanched almonds
½ tsp salt
1 tsp almond essence
150 grams melted butter

1. Put the flour, caster sugar, almonds and salt into a food processor and pulse to coarsely chop the almonds and mix ingredients together.
2. With the motor running, pour the almond essence and melted butter down the feed tube as fast as the dry ingredients can absorb it.
3. Once all the butter has been added, pulse the mix until the mixture becomes like coarse crumbs.
4. Press the mixture into a greased, floured and paper-lined 23 cm square cake tin.
5. Bake at 180°C for 20 minutes or until the shortbread begins to brown.
6. Cool in the tin. Break into odd-shaped pieces to serve with coffee. Store in an airtight container.

Orange coconut shortbread

60 small or 30 large pieces

200 grams butter
½ cup caster sugar
2 tsp grated orange rind
2 cups flour
½ tsp salt
½ cup coconut

1. Beat the butter, sugar and orange rind together until light and creamy. Do this in a food processor or by hand.
2. Sift the flour and salt together and work into the creamed mixture with the coconut.
3. Turn the dough out onto a floured board and knead together.
4. Roll the dough out to 0.5 cm thickness and cut into shapes. Place on a greased baking tray.
5. Bake at 180°C for 15 minutes or until lightly golden and firm. Cool on the tray for 10 minutes before transferring to a cake rack to cool. Store in an airtight container.

Cook's Tip:

I do not prepare this recipe in the food processor as the coconut will be milled too finely. It will work well enough in the processor though so do use it if you are short of time.

With added oat bran for an even nuttier texture, these shortbread are particularly delicious.

Wholemeal shortbread

30-35 pieces

275 grams unsalted butter
½ cup firmly packed brown sugar
1 cup flour
1½ cups wholemeal flour
½ cup oat bran
½ tsp salt

If you have no oatbran use all wholemeal flour.

1. Put the butter and brown sugar into a food processor and process until well mixed and light.
2. Add the flour, wholemeal flour, oat bran and salt and process until the mixture is combined.
3. Turn out onto a floured board and bring together. Knead lightly.
4. Roll out to 1–1.5 cm thickness and cut into finger-shaped bars. Place on a greased baking tray.
5. Bake at 180°C for 25 minutes or until firm to the touch and lightly browned.
6. Cool on the tray for 10 minutes before transferring to a cake rack. Store in an airtight container.

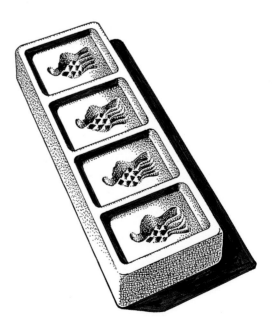

CAKES

The greatest satisfaction to me in baking is turning out the perfect cake. I love all aspects of baking, but probably because it has taken time to master the art of cakes I now feel great pride creating a wonderful cake. Cakes were regularly prepared in my home as a child but it has taken time and practice to master the skills so inherent in my mother. Her Tea Cake was served hot and well buttered most weekends. Christmas cakes were dark, moist and rich. And the basic butter cake was miraculously turned into chocolate, lemon, rainbow and many other variations with what seemed little effort.

Preparing cakes back then was time consuming. As today we are often 'time poor', I have made most of the following recipes using the food processor, though hand beater instructions have been added at the end of most of the recipes too. To some degree when using a food processor we have to balance its speed against the old-fashioned texture that comes from the traditional creaming method. I maintain that the difference is more than acceptable, and on occasions even better.

From the Melt 'n' Mix Banana Cake to John's Turkish Orange Cake, I am sure there will be something in this chapter that you will enjoy.

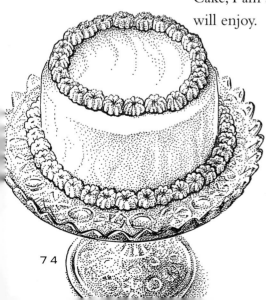

One of my favourite flavours. You can ice the cake if wished.

Butterscotch cake

2 eggs
1 cup soft brown sugar
1 tblsp golden syrup
1 tsp vanilla essence
150 grams butter

1½ cups self rising flour
½ tsp ground cinnamon
½ cup milk
70-gram pkt walnut halves

1. Put the eggs, soft brown sugar, golden syrup and vanilla essence into a food processor and process for 2 minutes until light and creamy.
2. Add the butter and process a further 2 minutes.
3. Add the flour and cinnamon together and pulse into the creamed mixture with the milk.
4. Turn the mixture into a greased, floured and lined 20 cm cake tin. Decorate the top with the walnuts.
5. Bake at 180°C for 40-45 minutes.
6. Cool in the tin for 10 minutes before turning out onto a cake rack to cool. If wished, ice with butterscotch icing. Store in an airtight container.

Butterscotch icing

1 cup soft brown sugar
¼ cup milk
1 tsp vanilla essence

Put all ingredients in a saucepan and bring to the boil. Stir over a gentle heat and simmer for 5 minutes. Remove from the heat and beat until the mixture thickens and cools.

Hand/electric beater method

Beat the butter, sugar and golden syrup together until light and creamy. Add the eggs and vanilla and beat well. Sift the flour and fold into the creamed mixture alternately with the milk. Continue from step 4.

Apple and lemon teacake

This is best served warm in wedges and lightly buttered.

½ cup brown sugar
2 eggs
75 grams butter
grated rind of 1 lemon
1¼ cups self rising flour
pinch of salt

¼ cup milk
1 apple
1 tblsp extra butter
1 tblsp caster sugar
½ tsp ground cinnamon

1. Put the sugar and eggs into a food processor and process for 2 minutes.
2. Add the butter and lemon rind and process for a further 2 minutes until creamy.
3. Add the flour, salt and milk and pulse to mix. Do not over process.
4. Turn mixture into a greased, floured and lined 20 cm round cake tin.
5. Peel, core and finely slice the apple and arrange decoratively on top.
6. Bake at 180°C for 25–30 minutes or until a skewer inserted comes out clean.
7. Allow the cake to stand in the tin 10 minutes before turning out onto a cake rack to cool. Spread with the 1 tablespoon extra butter and sprinkle over the sugar and cinnamon. Serve warm. Store in an airtight container.

Hand/electric beater method

Cream together the butter, sugar and lemon rind until light and fluffy. Add the eggs and beat well. Sift the flour and salt together and fold into the creamed mixture alternately with the milk. Continue from step 4.

Golden sour cream cake

This cake is not dissimilar to my childhood favourite, Golden Syrup Pudding.

¼ cup golden syrup
200 grams softened butter
¼ cup finely chopped walnuts
½ cup caster sugar
1 egg
2 cups pure flour
½ tsp ground ginger

½ tsp ground cinnamon
2 tsp baking powder
pinch salt
½ tsp baking soda
250-gram tub sour cream
¼ cup lemon juice
icing sugar

1. Mix together two tablespoons of the golden syrup and two tablespoons of softened butter and spread liberally over the base of a 23 cm ring cake tin. Cover with the chopped walnuts. Grease the sides.
2. Put the remaining butter, sugar and egg into a food processor and process for 2 minutes until light.
3. Add the flour, ginger, cinnamon, baking powder, salt and baking soda and pulse into the creamed mixture with the sour cream and lemon juice.
4. Pour the cake mixture into the prepared cake tin.

5. Bake at 180°C for 45 minutes or until a skewer inserted comes out clean.
6. Cool in the tin for 5 minutes before turning out onto a cake rack to cool. Dust with icing sugar to serve. Store in an airtight container.

Hand/electric beater method
To make the cake, beat together the butter and sugar until light and creamy. Add the egg and beat well. Sift together the flour, ginger, cinnamon, baking powder, salt and baking soda. Fold the dry ingredients into the creamed mixture alternately with the sour cream and lemon juice. Continue from step 4.

Frangipani cake

A soft-textured cake topped with a coconut meringue. This recipe hails from my home town, Launceston, in Tasmania.

¾ cup caster sugar
3 eggs (2 separated, 1 whole)
1 tsp vanilla essence
grated rind of 1 orange
175 grams butter

1½ cups self rising flour
¼ cup milk
½ cup caster sugar
1 cup coconut

1. Put the first measure of sugar, 2 egg yolks and 1 whole egg, vanilla essence and orange rind into a food processor and process for 2-3 minutes.
2. Add the butter and process until well combined.
3. Add the flour and milk and pulse to blend. Do not over process.
4. Turn the mixture into a greased, floured and lined 20 cm cake tin.
5. In a clean bowl beat the 2 egg whites until they are stiff but not dry. Add the second measure of sugar and beat until dissolved. Add the coconut and spread the mixture on top of the cake.
6. Bake at 180°C for 40-45 minutes or until a skewer inserted comes out clean. Be careful as the centre takes a deceptively long time to cook.
7. Stand in the tin 10 minutes before cooling on a cake rack. Store in an airtight container.

Hand/electric beater method
Beat the first measure of sugar and butter until light and creamy. Add the 2 egg yolks, whole egg, vanilla essence and orange rind and beat well. Fold in the sifted flour alternately with the milk. Continue from step 4.

Cook's Tip:
Adding a pinch of cream of tartar to the egg whites will help them gain greater volume.

Kevin's gingerbread

Kevin is a good friend and even game enough to tell me when he thinks my gingerbread needs more ginger. So just for Kevin (sweet-tooth fanatic), I have added extra ginger.

1 cup soft brown sugar
1 egg
125 grams butter
½ cup golden syrup
¾ cup milk
2½ cups pure flour

1½ tblsp ground ginger
pinch salt
1 tsp baking soda
1 tsp cinnamon
3-4 pieces crystallized ginger

Cook's Tip:

In place of the crystallized ginger, when cold ice with lemon icing.

1. Beat the sugar and egg together in a food processor.
2. Melt the butter and golden syrup together and stir in the milk. Cool.
3. Pulse in the flour, ground ginger, salt, baking soda and cinnamon with the cooled milk mixture.
4. Turn the mixture into a greased, floured and lined 20 cm round cake tin. Finely slice the crystallized ginger and sprinkle on top.
5. Bake at 180°C for 35-40 minutes or until a cake skewer inserted comes out clean.
6. Allow to stand in the tin for 10 minutes before turning out onto a cake rack to cool. Store in an airtight container.

American strawberry shortcake

Fresh season strawberries folded into whipped cream and sandwiched between a rich shortcake are a great treat.

2½ cups self rising flour
½ cup sugar
pinch salt
125 grams cream cheese
50 grams butter

1 egg
2 tblsp sour cream
¾ cup cream
2 tblsp melted butter

Filling
1 punnet strawberries
2 tblsp orange liqueur
300-ml bottle cream
icing sugar

1. Put the flour, sugar and salt into a food processor and pulse to mix.
2. Add the cream cheese and the first measure of butter, and process until the mixture resembles crumbs.
3. Beat the egg, sour cream and cream together until just combined and pulse into the mixture until it forms a soft dough.
4. Divide the dough into two equal parts and press one half into a greased, floured and lined 23 cm cake tin. Press the remaining half out to a 23 cm

circle on a lightly floured board. Place the second half on top of the half already in the cake tin.

5. Drizzle the melted butter over the top of the cake.

6. Bake at 220°C for 15 minutes. Turn the oven down to 150°C and continue to cook a further 20-25 minutes until firm to the touch.

7. To serve: split the cake in half. It will split easily where the two pieces were placed on top of each other. Hull and slice the strawberries. Toss in the liqueur and leave for 5 minutes. Whip the cream and sweeten with icing sugar to your taste. Fill the centre with half the strawberries and whipped cream. Cover with the second layer of shortcake and top with the remaining strawberries and cream. Serve fresh.

Apple slice cake

2 eggs
1 cup caster sugar
250 grams butter
2 cups self rising flour
1 tsp lemon essence

½ tsp ground nutmeg
1 tsp ground cinnamon
½ cup milk
1 cup stewed apples (not too wet)

1. Put the eggs and sugar into a food processor and process until the mixture is light.

2. Add the butter and process a further 2 minutes until creamy.

3. Sprinkle the flour, lemon essence, nutmeg and cinnamon evenly over the creamed mixture. Pour over the milk and pulse to mix.

4. Spread half the cake mixture into a greased, floured and lined 20 cm loose-bottomed cake tin. Spread over the apples and carefully cover the apples with the remaining cake mixture.

5. Bake at 180°C for 30 minutes or until a skewer inserted comes out clean.

6. Stand in the tin for 10 minutes before turning out onto a cake rack to cool. Top with whipped cream for a special occasion or simply decorate with a dusting of icing sugar. Store in an airtight container.

Hand/electric beater method

Beat the butter, sugar and golden syrup together until light and creamy. Add the eggs and vanilla and beat well. Sift the flour and fold into the creamed mixture alternately with the milk. Continue from step 4.

Gingerbread by Norma

This recipe, from my aunt, is made with a large percentage of water, which makes the cake particularly light. It is also beautifully moist and keeps well in an airtight container.

125 grams butter
2 tblsp sugar
1 egg
1 cup golden syrup
2¼ cups pure flour

1 tsp baking powder
½ tsp salt
1 tsp ground cinnamon
1 tsp ground ginger
1 cup cold water

1. Put the butter, sugar and egg into a food processor and process until creamy.
2. With the motor running, pour the golden syrup down the feed tube.
3. Sift the flour, baking powder, salt, cinnamon and ginger together, and sprinkle evenly on top of the mixture in the food processor.
4. Pour the water on top of the flour. Pulse all the ingredients together. Do not over mix or turn on to full speed and forget.
5. Pour the mixture into a well greased, floured and lined 23 cm round cake tin.
6. Bake at 180°C for 40–45 minutes or until a skewer inserted comes out clean.
7. Cool in the tin for 10 minutes before turning out onto a cake rack to cool. Ice with lemon icing when cold, or dust with icing sugar. Store in an airtight container.

Variations:
- Use half wholemeal and half plain flour.
- Use ground cardamom instead of cinnamon.

Hand/electric beater method
Beat the butter and sugar together until light and creamy. Add the egg and beat well. Carefully blend in the golden syrup, cold water and sifted dry ingredients. Blend together with a holed spoon. Do not over mix. Continue from step 5.

Opposite: Chocolate Fudge Cake (page 157).

Pear and walnut cake

When ripe, pears are full of flavour. They are more distinctive than apples and in this recipe make a delightful cake to take on a picnic.

2 pears	*pinch ground nutmeg and ground*
2 eggs	*cinnamon*
½ cup sugar	*½ cup melted butter*
¼ cup self rising flour	*½ cup chopped walnuts*
1 heaped tblsp wholemeal self rising flour	

1. Wash the pears, peel and dice.
2. Put the eggs and sugar into a food processor and process for 2 minutes or until light.
3. Sprinkle in the sifted flours, nutmeg and cinnamon and pulse to mix. Pulse in the melted butter.
4. Pour mixture into a greased, floured and lined 20 cm round cake tin. Half submerge the fruit diagonally into the mixture and arrange nuts on top.
5. Bake in a 180°C oven for 1 hour.
6. Allow to stand in the tin for 10 minutes before turning out onto a cake rack to cool. Store in an airtight container.

Hand/electric beater method

Beat the sugar and eggs together until the mixture is light and fluffy. Sift the flours with the spices and fold into the egg mixture with the melted butter. Continue from step 4.

Melt 'n' mix banana cake

Banana cakes are a real favourite and this one will be no exception. It is quick to make, with no need to cream or beat.

150 grams butter	*2 tsp baking powder*
¾ cup sugar	*½ tsp baking soda*
2 eggs	*½ cup milk*
1 tsp vanilla essence	*1 cup mashed banana*
2 cups pure flour	

1. Melt the butter. Add the sugar, eggs and vanilla, and mix well.
2. Sift the flour, baking powder and soda together into a bowl and make a well in the centre.
3. Pour in the melted butter mixture and begin to mix carefully, adding the milk and banana at the same time.
4. Pour the mixture into a well greased and floured 20 cm ring tin.
5. Bake at 180°C for 30–40 minutes.
6. Allow to stand in the tin for 10 minutes before turning out onto a cake rack to cool. Ice with passionfruit icing. Store in an airtight container.

Opposite: Debbie's Chocolate Fudge Cake (page 163).

Orange and pumpkin cake

This is a wonderfully moist cake that is one of my favourites in this chapter.

1 cup sugar
2 eggs
grated rind 2 oranges
250 grams butter
1 cup wholemeal self rising flour

1 cup self rising flour
½ tsp cinnamon (optional)
½ cup fresh orange juice
1 cup cold mashed pumpkin

1. Put the sugar, eggs and orange rind into a food processor and process for 2 minutes until the mixture is light.
2. Add the butter and process until creamy.
3. Put the flours and cinnamon into the food processor with the orange juice and pumpkin. Pulse to blend. Do not over process.
4. Turn the mixture into a well greased, floured and lined 23 cm cake tin.
5. Bake at 160°C for 1–1¼ hours or until a skewer inserted comes out clean.
6. Allow to stand in the tin for 10 minutes before turning out onto a cake rack to cool. Ice with butter icing and decorate with grated orange rind. Store in an airtight container.

Cook's Tip:

Make sure the pumpkin is dry not wet.

Variations:

Add 1 cup chopped dates, prunes or apricots to the mixture if wished.

Hand/electric beater method

Beat the butter, sugar and orange rind together until light and creamy. Add the eggs and beat well. Sift together the flours and cinnamon and return any husks to the bowl. Blend the flours into the creamed mixture with the mashed pumpkin and orange juice. Continue from step 4.

Honey cake

Richly flavoured with honey, this is a super cake. The recipe comes from my sister-in-law Joan in Tasmania.

150 grams butter
1 cup creamed honey
¼ cup caster sugar
1 tsp lemon essence
1 tsp vanilla essence
4 eggs

250-gram tub sour cream
2½ cups flour
1 tsp baking soda
1 tsp baking powder
pinch salt

1. Put the butter, honey, sugar, essences and eggs into a food processor and process until the mixture is light. This will take about 3–4 minutes.
2. Add the sour cream and process a further minute.
3. Sift the flour, baking soda, baking powder and salt and sprinkle over the top of the creamed mixture. Pulse to blend. Do not over process.

4. Turn the mixture into a greased and floured 23 cm round ring tin.

5. Bake at 180°C for 45-50 minutes or until a skewer inserted comes out clean.

6. Cool in the tin for 10 minutes before turning out onto a cake rack to cool. Store in an airtight container.

Variation:

Remove 1 cup of the plain flour and substitute 1 cup wholemeal.

Hand/electric beater method

Beat the butter, honey and sugar together until light and creamy. Add the lemon and vanilla essence and the eggs one at a time; beat well after each addition. Beat in the sour cream. Sift together the dry ingredients and gently blend into the creamed mixture with a holed spoon. Continue from step 4.

Raspberry upside-down cake

This version makes a refreshing change to pineapple upside-down cake.

125 grams unsalted butter
¾ cup caster sugar
300-gram pack free-flow frozen raspberries (defrosted)
1 egg
1 tsp vanilla essence
3 tblsp raspberry liqueur
1¼ cups self rising flour
¼ cup milk

Framboise is raspberry liqueur and you can buy very good raspberry eau de vie made from Nelson in miniatures. If you do not have it, use another liqueur such as Cointreau or Grand Marnier.

1. Take one tablespoon butter from the 125 grams and melt. Pour it over the base of a 23 cm cake tin. Take ¼ cup caster sugar from the ¾ cup and sprinkle over the butter. Arrange the raspberries on top and set the tin aside.

2. Put the remaining butter, sugar, egg, vanilla essence and liqueur into a food processor and process for about 1 minute until light.

3. Add the sifted flour and pulse into the creamed mixture with the milk. Do not over process.

4. Spread the batter over the fruit.

5. Bake at 180°C for 30 minutes or until a skewer inserted comes out clean.

6. Invert the cake onto a cake rack to cool. Serve for afternoon tea with whipped cream. This cake is best eaten on the day it is made.

Hand/electric beater method

For the cake, beat together the butter and sugar until the mixture is light and creamy. Add the egg and vanilla essence and beat well. Fold in the sifted flour alternately with the milk. Continue from step 4.

Citrus syrup cake

2 oranges
1 cup caster sugar
3 eggs

125 grams butter
1¼ cups pure flour
1½ tsp baking powder

Syrup
3 tblsp orange juice
2 tblsp sieved apricot jam
2 tblsp sugar

1. Pare the rind from orange and squeeze the juice. Put the sugar and orange rind into a food processor fitted with the metal blade. Process until the orange rind is finely chopped.
2. Add the eggs and process until pale and thick.
3. Add the softened butter and process until creamy.
4. Sift the flour and baking powder together and sprinkle the flour evenly on top of the butter mixture. Pour over the orange juice.
5. Pulse to mix.
6. Turn into a greased and floured 20 cm ring tin.
7. Bake at 180°C for 35 minutes or until a skewer inserted comes out clean.
8. Drizzle the syrup over the top. Cool in the tin for 10 minutes before turning out onto a cake rack to cool. Store in an airtight container.

Syrup
Put the orange juice, apricot jam and sugar into a small bowl and heat in the microwave until the sugar has dissolved. Alternatively heat in a saucepan and stir until the sugar has dissolved.

Hand/electric beater method
Grate the rind from the orange and squeeze the juice. Beat the butter and sugar together until the mixture is light and creamy. Add the eggs and beat well. Sift the flour and baking powder together and fold into the creamed mixture alternately with the orange juice. Continue from step 6.

Cook's Tip:

Always use the pulse button when mixing flour into creamed mixtures in the food processor. Do not put on full power as it will make a tough textured cake with little rise.

This is quick to make and delicious to eat as a dessert or just with coffee. Seasonal variations can be made according to the fruit available.

Peach struesel cake

2 eggs
¾ cup caster sugar
125 grams butter
1½ cups self rising flour

2 tblsp custard powder
½ cup milk
1 cup sliced peaches

Topping
½ cup flour
½ cup raw sugar
¼ cup coconut
75 grams butter

1. Put the eggs and sugar into a food processor and process for 2 minutes or until light.
2. Add the butter and process until light, about another 2 minutes.
3. Add the flour, custard powder and milk together and pulse until just combined. Do not over process.
4. Turn the mixture into a well greased, floured and lined 20 cm loose-bottomed cake tin. Arrange the peaches on the top of the batter. Sprinkle over the topping.
5. Bake at 180°C for about 1 hour or until a skewer inserted comes out clean.
6. Stand in the tin for 10 minutes before turning out onto a cake rack to cool. Store in an airtight container.

Topping
Mix the flour, sugar and coconut together. Rub in the butter until the mixture resembles fine crumbs.

Variations:
• Use rhubarb and ground ginger.
• Tinned apples with mixed spice.
• Peeled and sliced feijoas with ginger.

Hand/electric beater method
Beat the butter and sugar together until light and creamy. Add the eggs and beat well. Sift together the flour and custard powder and fold into the creamed mixture alternately with the milk. Continue from step 4.

Apple cake

50 grams butter
1 cup sugar
2 eggs
4 apples

2 cups flour
2 tsp baking soda
1 tsp nutmeg
2 tsp cinnamon

1. Melt butter in a large bowl or saucepan.
2. Add sugar and eggs and mix well.
3. Peel and core apples. Slice thinly.
4. Add apples, flour, baking soda, nutmeg and cinnamon to mixture. Stir until mixed and turn into a greased 20 cm square cake tin.
5. Bake at 180°C for 50 minutes.
6. Just before serving sprinkle with icing sugar. Store in an airtight container.

Swedish cardamom picnic cake

Cardamom is widely used in the cooking of Scandinavian countries. This cake is another quick one to make, and is ideal to rustle up in a hurry for an outing like a picnic.

1 egg
¾ cup caster sugar
2 tsp ground cardamom
75 grams softened butter

¾ cup cream
½ cup milk
2 cups self rising flour
70-gram pkt flaked almonds

Topping
¼ cup coffee crystals (sugar)
¼ cup pure flour
25 grams butter
grated rind of 1 lemon

Cook's Tip:

Cardamom is a strong spice, so tread carefully until you have mastered its strength. If you do not have any, use ground ginger in this recipe. The flavour will change but be just as good.

1. Put the egg, sugar and cardamom into a food processor and process for 2 minutes until light.
2. Add the butter and process for a further 2 minutes.
3. Add the cream, milk and flour and pulse to blend. Do not over process.
4. Turn the mixture into a well greased, floured and lined 23 cm round cake tin. Sprinkle the almonds on top and push in using a fork. Sprinkle the topping over the almonds.
5. Bake at 180°C for 45-50 minutes or until a cake skewer inserted comes out clean.
6. Cool in the tin for 10 minutes before transferring to a cake rack. Store in an airtight container.

Topping
Put the coffee crystals, flour, lemon rind and butter in a food processor and pulse to blend well.

Hand/electric beater method

Beat the butter and sugar together until light and creamy. Add the egg and beat well. Sift together the flour and ground cardamom and fold into the creamed mixture. Continue from step 4.

Carrot cake

Carrot cakes have been around for ages, but they still seem to be popular. I'm sure this is because we think we are being half-good if a cake has carrots and wholemeal flour in it! We do fool ourselves a lot, don't we! Carrot cake is exceptionally calorific, but it's wonderful (occasionally)!

100 grams melted butter
½ cup light tasteless oil
½ cup honey
2 eggs
1 tsp vanilla essence
¾ cup pure flour
¾ cup wholemeal flour

1 tsp baking soda
1 tsp baking powder
¼ tsp each ground cloves, cinnamon,
*   nutmeg, ginger and cardamom*
1½ cups grated carrot
½ cup chopped pecans
½ cup sultanas

Cream cheese icing

½ cup cream cheese
1 cup icing sugar
1 tsp vanilla essence

1 tsp honey
milk

1. In a large bowl beat together the butter, oil, honey, eggs and vanilla essence.
2. Add the pure flour, wholemeal flour, baking soda, baking powder, spices, carrot, pecans and sultanas, and mix together well.
3. Pour into a well greased, floured and lined 20 cm loose-bottomed cake tin.
4. Bake at 180°C for 60–70 minutes or until a skewer inserted comes out clean.
5. Stand in the tin for 30 minutes before turning out onto a cake rack to cool. Ice with cream cheese icing. Store in an airtight container.

Cream cheese icing

Beat the cream cheese with the icing sugar, vanilla essence and honey. Mix with a little milk until smooth.

Variation:

Make the icing with ricotta cheese to cut down on the calories.

Try courgette and carrot or even grated pumpkin.

Jewel cake

I made this recipe for the first Christmas issue of *Next* magazine. It looks fabulous and makes a wonderful cake for a celebration.

150-gram packet glacé cherries
1 cup sultanas
½ cup raisins
½ cup brandy, stout or orange juice
grated rind 2 lemons
1 tsp mixed spice

1 tsp ground cardamom
½ cup brown sugar
2 eggs
100 grams butter
1¼ cups pure flour

Topping

about ½ cup redcurrant jelly
1½ cups whole nuts (Brazil, almonds,
   hazelnuts and/or walnuts)

½ cup glacé fruits
cachous
whole glacé cherries with stalks

1. In a bowl combine the glacé cherries, sultanas, raisins, brandy, lemon rind and spices. Cover and leave overnight.
2. Put the sugar and eggs into a food processor and process for 2-3 minutes until light. Add the butter and process a further 2 minutes.
3. Sprinkle over the sifted flour and the fruit mixture. Pulse to mix.
4. Turn into a greased and floured 20 cm ring tin.
5. Bake at 170°C for about 50 minutes, until a skewer inserted comes out clean.
6. Cool in the tin for 10 minutes before turning out onto a cake rack to cool. Decorate when cold. Store in an airtight container.

Topping

Heat the redcurrant jelly. Toss the whole nuts and glacé fruit (except the whole cherries) in the jelly. Arrange the nuts on the top of the cake. Quickly flash the cake under a hot grill to slightly caramelise the topping. Decorate with cachous and whole cherries.

Hand/electric beater method

Beat the butter and sugar together until light and creamy. Add the eggs and beat well. Sift the flour and sprinkle over the creamed mixture. Carefully blend in with the fruit mixture. Continue from step 4.

Cook's Tip:

Use glacé cherries without stalks if whole cherries with stalks are unavailable.

The ricotta chocolate filling in this cake makes it special and an ideal treat for a summer luncheon.

Ricotta cake

3 cups pure flour
1 tblsp baking powder
½ cup brown sugar
1 cup ground almonds

250 grams butter (well chilled)
2 eggs, beaten
2 tsp almond essence

Filling
750 grams ricotta cheese
½ cup grated dark chocolate
½ cup toasted pinenuts

1 cup mixed dried fruit
1 tsp vanilla essence

1. Put the flour, baking powder, brown sugar and almonds in a food processor. Pulse to sift.
2. Add the butter and process until the mixture resembles fine breadcrumbs.
3. Add the beaten eggs and almond essence and pulse to mix. The mixture will be crumbly.
4. Line a 23 or 25 cm cake tin with foil. Press half the crumble mixture into the base of the tin. Spread the filling on top and then cover filling with remaining crumble mixture. Press down firmly.
5. Bake at 180°C for 1 hour. (A 25 cm cake will take about 50 minutes.)
6. Cool in the tin for 10 minutes before transferring to a cake rack. When ready to serve, cover with a thick layer of sifted icing sugar. Store in the refrigerator.

Filling
Sieve or process the ricotta cheese until smooth. Pulse in the chocolate, pinenuts, dried fruit and vanilla essence.

By hand
Instead of using the food processor to process the butter and dry ingredients, rub the butter in by hand. Beat the eggs lightly and mix in with a fork.

Cook's Tips:

You can successfully use ricotta spread in place of ricotta cheese. Also consider substituting cottage cheese or quark.
To add more flavour to the dried fruit, soak it in a little brandy for 30-40 minutes beforehand.

Semolina and almond cake

¾ cup caster sugar
4 eggs
100 grams butter
½ cup fine-ground semolina

70-gram pkt ground almonds
2 tblsp freshly squeezed lemon juice
1 tblsp finely grated lemon rind
pinch of salt

Filling
150 grams ricotta cheese
¼ cup caster sugar
½ cup cream
icing sugar, to decorate

Cook's Tip:

In place of ricotta, use cream cheese or plain whipped cream.

Semolina is a more coarsely ground wheat, normally durum, and gives a lovely texture to this cake.

1. Put the sugar and eggs into a food processor. Process for one minute. Add the butter and process until creamy.
2. Pulse in the semolina, ground almonds, lemon juice, rind and salt.
3. Pour into a well greased, floured and lined 20 cm round cake tin.
4. Bake at 180°C for 40 minutes, or until golden and springy to touch.
5. Stand in tin for 5-10 minutes before turning out onto a cake rack to cool.
6. Cut cake in half horizontally and spread with the ricotta mixture. Top with the remaining layer of cake. Dust with icing sugar. Store in an airtight container.

Filling
Beat ricotta, sugar and cream together until smooth and thick.

Hand/electric beater method
Beat the butter and sugar together until light and creamy. Add the eggs and beat well. Fold in the semolina and salt with the almonds, lemon juice and lemon rind. Continue from step 3.

Marseilles

This cake looks dense but is moist and delicious. Change the flavour of the cake with different jams. My favourites are apricot and raspberry.

2 eggs
½ cup caster sugar
½ tsp vanilla

175 grams butter
2 cups self rising flour
¼ cup apricot jam or raspberry jam

1. Cream eggs and sugar with vanilla in the food processor for 3 minutes.
2. Add butter and process a further minute until creamy.
3. Pulse in self rising flour. Mixture will be thick and heavy.
4. Spread half the mixture in a well greased and floured 20 cm round cake tin. Spread this with a thick layer of jam, then carefully cover with remaining cake mixture. Use a knife dipped in hot water to smooth the top. If liked, add an extra 2 tablespoons of milk to the batter for the top.

5. Bake at 180°C for 30-40 minutes until golden brown.
6. Stand in the tin for 5 minutes before turning out onto a cake rack to cool. Sprinkle with sifted icing sugar. Store in an airtight container.

Hand/electric beater method

Beat the butter and sugar together until the mixture is light and creamy. Add the eggs and vanilla essence, and beat well. Fold in the sifted flour. Continue from step 4.

Buttermilk cake

Buttermilk adds a light tang to foods and helps keep them moist. Try this cake topped with butter icing or whipped cream.

4 egg yolks	*1 cup caster sugar*
¾ cup buttermilk	*1 tblsp baking powder*
2 tsp vanilla or lemon essence	*pinch salt*
2 cups pure flour	*125 grams softened butter*

1. Mix together the egg yolks, buttermilk and vanilla or lemon essence.
2. Put the flour, caster sugar, baking powder and salt into the food processor and pulse to sift.
3. Add the buttermilk mixture and butter and process for 1 minute.
4. Transfer the batter to a well greased and lined 23 cm loose-bottomed cake tin.
5. Bake at 180°C for 35-40 minutes until the cake is cooked and is just beginning to pull away from the sides of the cake tin.
6. Allow the cake to stand for 10 minutes before turning out onto a cake rack to cool. Serve cold. Store in an airtight container.

Variations:

* Add 1 teaspoon grated lemon rind and ½ teaspoon ground ginger.
* Substitute 1 tablespoon Angostura Bitters for the vanilla or lemon essence.

Hand/electric beater method

Beat the butter, sugar and vanilla essence until the mixture is light and creamy. Add the egg yolks and beat well. Sift together the flour, baking powder and salt and fold into the creamed mixture with the buttermilk. Continue from step 4.

Buttermilk, originally, was the milk left over from making butter, though today, however, it is commercially available. Try with the Basic Pancakes too, buttermilk makes them ever so light.

John's Turkish orange cake

I'm not sure who John is, but I found this amongst my mother's collection of recipes. It is truly wonderful and so simple to make. It's particularly good for a late afternoon tea session with friends.

2 large oranges (unpeeled)
6 eggs
1 cup caster sugar
2 tblsp lemon juice
1 tsp baking powder
4 × 70-gram pkt ground almonds

1. Put the unpeeled oranges in a saucepan. Cover with water and simmer for 1 hour. Drain and leave until thoroughly cold.
2. Cut the oranges into quarters and remove any pips. Put the oranges into a food processor and process until pulverized.
3. Add the eggs, sugar and lemon juice and process for 1 minute.
4. Add the baking powder and ground almonds and pulse to mix. Do not over process.
5. Pour into a well greased, floured and lined 23 cm cake tin.
6. Bake at 180°C for 50-60 minutes until golden in colour and a cake skewer inserted comes out clean.
7. Stand in the tin for 10 minutes before turning out onto a cake rack to cool. Serve dusted with icing sugar and accompanied with whipped cream. Store in an airtight container.

Coconut cake

1 cup hot milk
2 tblsp melted butter
4 eggs
1½ cups caster sugar
2 cups self rising flour
1 tsp vanilla essence
½ cup coconut

Topping
50 g butter
¼ cup brown sugar
2 tblsp cream
½ cup coconut (Shreds or flakes)

1. Mix the milk and butter together and set aside.
2. Put the eggs and sugar into a food processor and process for 2 minutes or until light.
3. Sprinkle in the sifted flour and pulse into the egg mixture with the hot milk, vanilla and coconut. Do not over process.
4. Turn the mixture into a well greased, floured and lined 20 cm round cake tin.
5. Bake at 180°C for 30-40 minutes or until a skewer inserted comes out clean.
6. Allow the cake to cool in the tin for 10 minutes before turning out onto a cake rack to cool.

Cook's Tip:

Coconut can go rancid. In fact quite often the desiccated coconut varieties we buy are already rancid. Store coconut in the freezer to keep it fresh.

7. Make up the topping and spread over the top of the cake. Place the cake under a medium grill for 3-5 minutes until the topping is browned. Watch it all the time and do not allow it to burn.

8. Cut into slices when cold. Store in an airtight container.

Topping

Melt butter and brown sugar together. Add the cream and stir in the coconut. Allow to cool and thicken slightly.

Hand/electric beater method

Combine the butter and milk and set aside. Beat the eggs and sugar together until they are light and creamy. Fold in the sifted dry ingredients and coconut alternately with the warm milk. Continue from step 4.

Toasted almond butter cake

The addition of toasted almonds and buttermilk to this cake makes it really different without much trouble. It freezes well too. Freeze while still warm.

70-gram pkt ground almonds
2 eggs
1 cup caster sugar
½ tsp almond essence
½ tsp vanilla essence

150 grams butter
2 cups self rising flour
1 tsp baking powder
½ tsp baking soda
¾ cup buttermilk

*Dense and moist —
you'll love this cake,
and it's so easy!*

1. Lightly toast the almonds in a non-stick pan over a moderate heat, shaking regularly to avoid them catching and burning.

2. Put the eggs, sugar, almond and vanilla essences into a food processor and process for 3 minutes until light.

3. Add the butter and process a further minute until the mixture is light.

4. Sprinkle over the sifted flour, baking powder and baking soda, cooled ground almonds and buttermilk.

5. Pulse until all the ingredients are combined. Do not over process.

6. Spread mixture into a well greased and floured 23 cm ring tin.

7. Bake at 180°C for 30-35 minutes until the cake is cooked.

8. Stand in the tin for 10 minutes before turning out onto a cake rack to cool. Serve dusted with icing sugar. Store in an airtight container.

Hand/electric beater method

Toast the almonds. Beat the butter, sugar, vanilla essence and almond essence to a cream. Add the eggs and beat well. Fold in the sifted dry ingredients with the buttermilk. Continue from step 6.

Mum's tea cake

This is my favourite cake. Well, yes, they're all favourites, but this is one my mother has always made and still does when I go home. It brings back warm memories of good family times and for this reason it is very special as my family are now far from me. I have never mastered the technique of making this in the food processor so the instructions are as Mum makes it!

50 grams softened butter
¾ cup caster sugar
1 egg

1½ cups self rising flour
¾ cup milk

Topping
1 tblsp softened butter
2 tblsp extra sugar
½ tsp cinnamon

When I was a kid butter was tops! In fact it was never considered that you shouldn't O.D. on it. Today we need to watch how much fat we eat, but some things don't taste right without butter and this tea cake is one. Enjoy it occasionally — winter time is best.

1. Mix the butter and sugar together in a bowl with a wooden spoon. There is not enough here to cream so mix as well as you can.
2. Beat in the egg.
3. Sift the flour and fold into the butter mixture alternately with the milk.
4. Spoon the batter into a well greased and floured 20 cm loose-bottomed cake tin.
5. Bake at 180°C for 40 minutes.
6. Allow the cake to stand in the tin for 5 minutes, then turn out onto a cake rack to cool.
7. While the cake is still hot, spread the top with the extra butter and sprinkle over the sugar and cinnamon. Serve warm spread with butter. Store in an airtight container.

Washington currant pound cake

Traditional and good. This is a standby recipe for taking on the annual holiday that improves on keeping. I recommend making this with the traditional 'cream butter and sugar' method.

3½ cups pure flour
1½ tsp baking powder
1 tsp freshly grated nutmeg
½ tsp salt
375 grams unsalted butter

2 cups caster sugar
6 eggs
1½ tsp vanilla essence
1 cup milk
2 cups currants

1. Sift the flour, baking powder, nutmeg and salt. Set aside.
2. Cream the butter and sugar.
3. Add the eggs, one at a time, beating well after each addition. Add the vanilla and continue beating until the mixture is smooth, light and fluffy.
4. Fold one-third of the flour mixture into the creamed mixture with a holed spoon and add one-third of the milk.

5. Repeat with remaining flour and milk. Mix only until ingredients are combined.
6. Fold in currants and turn into greased and floured 25 cm ring tin.
7. Bake at 180°C oven for 1 hour and 20 minutes, or until a skewer inserted comes out clean.
8. Allow to cool in the tin for 15 minutes before turning out onto a cake rack to cool. Store in an airtight container for 3 days before serving.

Coffee syrup cake

This is ideal to enjoy with coffee. A light butter-style cake is soaked in a coffee syrup and dusted with icing sugar to serve. It looks and tastes great.

3 eggs
¾ cup caster sugar
175 grams butter
1¼ cups self rising flour

¼ cup fresh white breadcrumbs
pinch salt
2 tblsp cream or milk

Syrup
1½ cups strong black coffee
½ cup sugar
1 tsp vanilla essence or 1 tblsp coffee liqueur

1. Put the eggs and sugar into a food processor and process until light.
2. Add the softened butter and process until thick and creamy.
3. Add the flour, breadcrumbs, salt and cream or milk and process a further 30 seconds to mix well.
4. Transfer the batter into a well greased and floured kugelhopf tin or 23 cm ring tin.
5. Bake at 190°C for 40 minutes or until a skewer inserted comes out clean.
6. Allow to stand in the tin for 10 minutes then turn the cake out onto a cake rack and allow to cool completely.
7. Return the cake to the tin and pour the syrup over evenly. Allow the cake to stand 10 minutes before turning out onto a cake platter. Store in an airtight container.

Syrup
Put the coffee, sugar and vanilla essence or liqueur into a saucepan and heat until the sugar has dissolved. Do not boil.

Hand/electric beater method
Beat the butter and sugar until light and creamy. Add the eggs and beat well after each addition. Sift together the flour and salt and fold in alternately with the milk and cream. Continue from step 4.

Banana cake with walnut topping

125 grams butter
1 cup caster sugar
2 eggs

3 bananas
2 cups self rising flour
¼ cup milk

Topping
2 tblsp butter
¼ cup brown sugar
¼ cup walnut pieces
½ tsp cinnamon

Cook's Tips:

Cake may be cooked in a 23 cm ring tin. Cooking time will be 25-30 minutes.
Use sliced almonds instead of walnuts in the topping.

1. Place softened butter, caster sugar and eggs in food processor. Process until smooth. Add bananas and process until well combined.
2. Add flour and milk and pulse only until flour is just mixed in. Do not over process.
3. Spread into a greased, floured and lined 20 cm round cake tin.
4. Sprinkle with topping and bake at 180°C for 40 minutes or until cake is cooked. Store in an airtight container.

Topping
Melt butter. Combine butter, brown sugar, walnuts and cinnamon.

Hand/electric beater method
Beat the butter and sugar until light and creamy. Add the eggs and beat well. Mash the bananas and stir into the creamed mixture. Fold in the sifted flour alternately with the milk. Continue from step 3.

Mini Christmas cakes

12 cakes

These are ideal for giving away as Christmas gifts. They taste great and look wonderful.

175 grams unsalted butter
½ cup caster sugar
grated rind of 1 orange
2 eggs
1¾ cups flour

1½ tsp baking powder
¾ tsp ground cardamom (or ginger)
2 cups chopped dried plump apricots
about ¼ cup sliced almonds to garnish
 (optional)

Icing
1 cup icing sugar
orange juice
1 tsp grated orange or lemon rind

1. Cream the butter, sugar and orange rind until light.
2. Beat in the eggs one at a time.
3. Sift the flour, baking powder and cardamom together and fold into the creamed mixture with the dried fruit.
4. Divide mixture evenly between 12 well greased muffin moulds. Bake at

Opposite: Apple and Lemon Teacake (*at back*) (page 76), Mum's Tea Cake (page 94).

180°C for 16-20 minutes until cooked.

5. Cool on a wire rack before icing. Store in an airtight container.

Icing

Sift the icing sugar into a bowl. Stir in sufficient orange juice to make a thick icing. Add grated orange or lemon rind. Spread on top of Mini Christmas Cakes and garnish with almonds.

White velvet cake

This is a lovely soft cake made without egg yolks, just egg whites; the butter and vanilla give it a wonderful flavour. This cake will freeze well. Freeze while still warm.

4 egg whites	*1 tsp vanilla essence*
1 cup caster sugar	*3 cups self rising flour*
175 grams soft butter	*1 cup milk*

1. Put the egg whites and sugar into a food processor and process for 3 minutes until white and thick (they will not be thick like a meringue so do not expect this to happen).
2. Add the butter and vanilla essence and process a further 2 minutes until it is a creamed mixture.
3. Sprinkle the sifted flour on top of the creamed mixture and then pour over the milk. Pulse only until the flour and milk are incorporated.
4. Spread mixture into a well greased, floured and lined 23 cm cake tin.
5. Bake at 180°C for approximately 45 minutes until the cake is cooked. Allow to stand in the tin for 10 minutes before transferring to a cake rack to cool. Serve dusted with icing sugar or with a lemon icing. Store in an airtight container.

Hand/electric beater method

Beat the egg whites, caster sugar, vanilla essence and butter together until thick and creamy. Fold in the sifted flour alternately with the milk. Continue from step 4.

I freeze my cakes before they are completely cold as I seem to get a better result on defrosting. Do not freeze them though when they are too warm.

Opposite (from top to bottom): Melt 'n' Mix Banana Cake (page 81), Citrus Syrup Cake (page 84), Louise's Chocolate Cake (page 152).

Date and orange cake

1 cup chopped dates
1 tsp grated orange rind
¼ cup orange juice
¾ cup water

125 grams butter
1 cup sugar
1 egg
2 cups self rising flour

Icing

1 cup icing sugar
about 2 tblsp orange juice

1. Place dates, orange rind, orange juice, water, butter and sugar in a saucepan. Heat gently until the butter has melted and the mixture has just begun to simmer.
2. Remove from heat and leave to cool slightly.
3. Add egg and flour. Stir until just mixed and turn into a greased and floured 20 cm ring tin.
4. Bake at 180°C for 30 minutes or until cake feels cooked when touched lightly.
5. Leave to cool for 10 minutes before removing from tin. When cool ice with orange icing. Store in an airtight container.

Orange icing
Combine icing sugar with sufficient orange juice to make a spreadable icing. Stir until smooth.

Cook's Tip:

Unsalted butter brings out a better flavour in baking. Use it if you have it.

SCONES

Don't ever think scones are dull and dreary — quite the contrary. Freshly made and smothered in jam and whipped cream (very decadent), warm scones will always be a favourite. Scones originated in Scotland, and are said to have taken their name from the Stone (or Scone) of Destiny where Scottish kings were once crowned. Sounds all very majestic for the humble scone, don't you think! Try these scones, in particular the wholemeal recipes that combine health with tradition.

Basic scones

12 scones

I find the best scones I make are those that are bashed together quickly but lightly — so don't be too calculated and see how you go!

The lighter the hand when making scones, the lighter the scones. Well, that's the saying anyway. From this basic recipe you can make your own variations.

2 cups pure flour   *50 grams butter*
4 tsp baking powder   *¾ cup milk*
½ tsp salt

1. Sift the flour, baking powder and salt into a large bowl.
2. Cut in the butter until the mixture resembles fine crumbs. Make a well in the centre.
3. Pour in the milk and mix quickly with a knife until the mixture forms a soft dough.
4. Turn out the dough onto a lightly floured board and knead lightly. Roll out or press out to 2 cm thickness. (Do not press too hard.)
5. Cut into 5 cm rounds or squares and place on a greased baking tray. Brush with milk to glaze.
6. Bake at 230°C for 10 minutes until cooked.
Serve warm and fresh.

Variations:
- Add 2 tablespoons sugar for sweet scones.
- Make the scones with half wholemeal flour and half plain flour.
- Add ½ cup dried mixed fruit with 2 tablespoons brown sugar.
- Leave out the butter and rub in ¼ cup peanut butter.

Cook's Tips:

Add 1 beaten egg and remove 3 tblsp milk. Beat egg and milk together well. Use self rising flour in place of flour and baking powder.

Ginger pear pinwheels

12 scones

Sweetened with pear and scented with ginger, this is a delightful variation on an old favourite.

3 cups self rising flour   *50 grams butter*
2 tblsp sugar   *about 1 cup milk*

Filling
1 pear   *1 tblsp sugar*
grated rind of one lemon *ground ginger to flavour*

1. Sift the flour into a large bowl and stir in the sugar.
2. Cut in the butter until the mixture resembles crumbs and make a well in the centre.

3. Pour in the milk and mix quickly with a knife to make a soft dough. You may need to add a little more milk.

4. Turn the dough out onto a floured board and knead lightly. Roll the dough out to a large rectangle about 0.5 cm thickness.

5. Spread the filling over the dough, leaving a 1 cm edge all the way around. Roll the dough up from the long edge and cut into 12 even pieces.

6. Place the rounds onto a lightly greased baking tray in a circular shape. (These can be cooked in a 25 cm round cake tin.)

7. Bake at 220°C for 15 minutes or until cooked. Serve warm and fresh.

Filling

Peel, core and purée the pear. Mix with the lemon rind, sugar and ginger to taste.

Wholemeal date scones

16 scones

Rustic in look, great on taste!

½ cup pure flour	1 cup chopped dates
4 tsp baking powder	2 tblsp brown sugar
½ tsp salt	1 egg
½ tsp mixed spice	about 1 cup milk
1½ cups wholemeal flour	oat bran to decorate
50 grams butter	

1. Sift the flour, baking powder, salt and mixed spice into a large bowl. Stir in the wholemeal flour and mix well.

2. Cut in the butter until the mixture resembles fine crumbs. Stir in the dates and brown sugar. Make a well in the centre.

3. Mix the egg and milk together and pour into the well. Mix quickly with a knife to make a soft dough, adding more milk if necessary.

4. Turn the mixture out onto a floured board and knead lightly. Press out 3 cm thick and cut into squares to a size of your choice.

5. Transfer to a greased baking tray and sprinkle the oat bran on top.

6. Bake at 220°C for about 15 minutes until cooked. Serve warm and fresh.

Cheese and bacon scones

12 scones

Try other spices like ginger and paprika or curry powder and cumin. Add 2–4 tblsp chopped fresh herbs too!

Always popular, especially around lunchtime on the weekend.

3 rashers bacon
2 spring onions
1 cup pure flour
4 tsp baking powder
¼ tsp ground nutmeg
½ tsp paprika
1 cup wholemeal flour
50 grams butter
1 cup grated cheese
1 cup milk

1. Cut the rind from the bacon and discard. Dice the flesh and cook until crisp. Trim and finely chop the spring onions.
2. Sift the flour, baking powder, nutmeg and paprika into a large bowl and then stir through the wholemeal flour.
3. Add the butter and rub in until well mixed. Stir in the bacon, spring onions and half the grated cheese.
4. Make a well in the centre and pour in the milk. Stir quickly with a knife to form a soft dough.
5. Turn out onto a floured board and knead lightly. Roll or press out to 3 cm thickness.
6. Cut into 5 cm rounds and place close together on a greased tray. Top with remaining cheese.
7. Bake at 220°C for about 12-15 minutes until the scones are cooked. Serve warm and fresh.

Cook's Tips:

You can drain the fat from the bacon if wished or toss it in with the other ingredients. The fat gives a lovely bacony flavour.
Scones should be placed close together on the tray. Have them almost touching before cooking.

Potato scones

20 scones

It is best to use sieved potatoes that have not been mashed with any other ingredients. Do not process potatoes as they will go gluggy.

Served with crispy bacon, tomatoes and hot coffee, these potato scones are particularly good for breakfast.

2 cups pure flour
4 tsp baking powder
1 tsp salt
50 grams butter
1 cup cold sieved potato
about 1 cup milk
3 tblsp melted butter

1. Sift the flour, baking powder and salt into a large bowl.
2. Cut in the butter and potato and make a well in the centre.
3. Pour in the milk and mix quickly with a knife to make a soft dough, adding more milk if necessary.
4. Turn the dough out onto a floured board and knead lightly.

5. Roll the dough out to 1 cm thickness and spread the top with half the melted butter. Fold the dough back on top.
6. Cut 3 cm rounds from the dough and place on a greased baking tray. Brush with the remaining butter.
7. Bake at 220°C for about 12-15 minutes until cooked. Serve warm and fresh.

Variation:
Add chopped fresh herbs, or herbs and 1-2 tblsp grated Parmesan cheese.

Cook's Tips:

I place a clean teatowel on a cake rack, put the hot scones on top then fold the teatowel over to cover the scones. Allow to stand for 5 minutes before eating.
Always glaze scones with a little milk to give nice brown tops.
Use self rising flour if wished.

Pumpkin scones

24 scones

Pumpkin makes delicious sweet scones that are best served with apricot jam and whipped cream.

3 cups self rising flour
1 tsp baking powder
1 tsp salt
1 cup dry mashed pumpkin
1 egg
¾–1 cups milk
extra milk to glaze

1. Sift the flour, baking powder and salt into a large bowl and make a well in the centre.
2. Mix the mashed pumpkin, egg and ¾ cup of milk together and pour into the well.
3. Using a knife, mix quickly to form a soft dough. Add more milk if required. Turn out onto a lightly floured board and knead lightly.
4. Roll out to 3 cm thickness and cut into 5 cm rounds. Place on a greased baking tray.
5. Bake at 220°C for 12-15 minutes or until cooked. Serve warm and fresh.

Cook's Tip:

To test if scones are cooked, take one from the centre of the tray and break it open. If it is cooked inside, remove the tray; if not, cook a little longer. Try another scone a few minutes later.

Buttermilk biscuits

24 small scones

Shorter than a traditional English-style scone, these American scones are called biscuits and are well worth trying. They make great partners for hearty casseroles and soups. Try them in place of bread.

4 cups self rising flour
1 tsp baking soda
1 tsp salt
1 tblsp sugar

125 grams butter
1¼ cups buttermilk
½ cup milk

1. Sift the flour, baking soda, salt and sugar into a large bowl.
2. Cut in the butter until the mixture resembles coarse crumbs.
3. Make a well in the centre and pour in the buttermilk and milk. Using a knife, mix quickly to form a soft dough. Add more milk if necessary.
4. Turn out onto a lightly floured board and knead lightly. Roll out mixture to 2 cm thickness. Cut into rounds and place on a greased baking tray.
5. Bake at 220°C for 15 minutes until well risen and golden. Serve warm and fresh.

Banana scones

20 scones

Bananas are a favourite fruit with New Zealanders. Try these for a yummy variation.

1 cup pure flour
4 tsp baking powder
¼ tsp salt
½ tsp ground allspice
1 cup wholemeal flour

50 grams butter
¼ cup raw sugar
2 medium sized bananas
about ½ cup milk
1-2 tblsp extra raw sugar

1. Sift the flour, baking powder, salt and allspice into a large bowl. Stir in the wholemeal flour and mix well.
2. Cut in the butter until the mixture resembles fine crumbs. Stir in the sugar.
3. Mash the bananas and stir into the flour mixture. Add enough milk to make a soft dough.
4. Turn out onto a lightly floured board and knead lightly. Roll out to about 3 cm thickness and cut into 5 cm rounds. Place on a greased baking tray and glaze with a little extra milk. Sprinkle the extra raw sugar on top.
5. Bake at 200°C for 15 minutes or until cooked and golden. These are most delicious served warm and fresh.

MUFFINS

There's nothing nicer than the smell of muffins cooking, then the joy of stealing one hot from the tray (they are best fresh and warm) without anyone noticing. Although the great hole left needs some explanation!

The best muffin I have ever tasted came from a small delicatessen in Remuera, Auckland. It was chocolate chip, and my disappointment was great if they were off the menu and something else was on when I went to get one for my morning tea! I was never able to wheedle the recipe out of the owner, but I have tried hard to recreate them here.

Muffins are easy for kids to make, and a basic recipe can accommodate any variation. Just remember not to over mix the batter, as this will cause the muffins to peak.

Enjoy!

Cook's Tips:

When a recipe calls for you to rub the butter into the flour until the mixture resembles fine crumbs, you can see if this point has been reached by giving the bowl a good shake. Any large pieces of butter will come to the top and can then be rubbed in easily.

Use 1 cup of self rising flour and 1 cup of self rising wholemeal flour and omit the baking powder if wished.

Best-ever bran and honey muffins

12 muffins

I am very tired of bran muffins that taste like chaff. Muffins are supposed to be soft and delicate, with good flavour — like these bran and honey muffins. Moist with a rich honey flavour, if you like bran muffins, you'll love these.

100 grams butter
½ cup brown sugar
½ cup liquid honey
2 eggs
grated rind 1 lemon
1½ cups flour

2 tsp baking soda
1 tsp baking powder
1 cup cooking bran
1 cup mixed dried fruit or sultanas
1½ cups buttermilk

Cook's Tip:

Do not over process or blend muffins; they will peak like mountains and be tough when cooked.

1. Put the butter, sugar, honey, eggs and lemon rind into a food processor and process until well combined.
2. Sift the flour, baking soda and baking powder into a bowl and stir through the bran and the fruit. Make a well in the centre.
3. Pour the butter mixture into the well with the buttermilk and fold ingredients together with a holed spoon.
4. Fill 12 greased muffin tins with the mixture.
5. Bake at 220°C for 15 minutes or until well risen. Serve warm.

Variation:
Make the recipe with half wheatgerm and half bran.

Chocolate berry muffins

12 muffins

Use your favourite berry — blueberries, raspberries and blackberries are best.

2 cups self rising flour
2 tblsp cocoa
¾ cup sugar
100 grams butter
1 tblsp golden syrup

¾ cup milk
1 tsp vanilla essence
1 egg
1-1½ cups berries (not loganberries)

1. Sift the flour and cocoa into a bowl. Stir in the sugar and make a well in the centre.
2. Melt the butter and golden syrup together. Add the milk, vanilla and egg and mix together.
3. Pour the liquid ingredients into the well and fold together with a holed spoon. Add the berries and fold through.
4. Fill 12 greased muffin tins with the mixture.
5. Bake at 220°C for 15 minutes or until well risen and golden.

Cook's Tip:

Heat the measuring spoon before measuring out the golden syrup to ensure the correct measure.

Variations:
- Substitute carob for cocoa.
- Use well drained and chopped tinned fruit.

I always enjoy savoury muffins. I have prepared these with soft blue cheese as I am not a lover of firm blue cheeses. To increase their flavour, fresh rosemary accentuates the cheese and olives.

1 cup flour
1 cup wholemeal flour
4 tsp baking powder
salt and pepper
50 grams butter
1 tblsp chopped rosemary

1/4 cup chopped olives (black or stuffed)
100 grams chopped soft blue cheese
1 egg
1 1/4 cups milk
1/4 cup grated cheddar cheese

1. Sift the flours, baking powder and good grindings of salt and pepper into a bowl, returning any husks to the bowl.
2. Rub in the butter, then stir in the rosemary, olives and blue cheese. Make a well in the centre.
3. Mix the egg and milk together, and pour in. Stir to mix only.
4. Fill 12 greased muffin tins with the mixture. Top each muffin with a little grated cheese.
5. Bake at 220°C for 15 minutes or until golden and cooked.
6. Butter and serve warm. Nice with smoked venison or beef.

Blue cheese and olive muffins

12 muffins

Try Ohua or Kikorangi cheese for this. They are my two favourite soft blue cheeses.

Richly flavoured with walnuts and golden syrup, these are best served hot and well buttered.

2 cups flour
1 tsp baking soda
2 tsp baking powder
pinch salt
1/4 cup sugar
70-gram pkt walnuts

75 grams melted butter
250-gram tub sour cream
1 egg
2 tblsp golden syrup
1/2 tsp vanilla essence

1. Sift the flour, baking soda, baking powder, salt and sugar into a large bowl.
2. Finely chop the walnuts and mix through. Make a well in the centre.
3. In a separate bowl mix together the butter, sour cream, egg, golden syrup and vanilla essence.
4. Pour the liquid ingredients into the well and fold through only until mixed.
5. Fill 12 greased muffin tins with the mixture.
6. Bake at 220°C for 15 minutes or until cooked.
7. Serve warm with butter and jam.

Variation:
Use pecans instead of walnuts.

Sour cream and walnut muffins

12 muffins

Cook's Tip:

Use a large slotted spoon when folding ingredients together. The holes will assist easy mixing.

Peach muffins

12 muffins

1 cup pure flour
1½ tsp ground cardamom
½ tsp ground ginger
1½ tsp baking powder
½ cup wholemeal flour
½ cup wheatgerm
3 tblsp sugar

2-3 peaches or 1 × 425-gram can
   peach slices
1 tblsp golden syrup
3 tblsp melted butter
¾ cup milk
1 egg

Topping
2 tsp finely chopped crystallized ginger
2 tblsp raw sugar

1. Sift the flour, cardamom, ginger and baking powder into a bowl. Add the wholemeal flour, wheatgerm and sugar, and mix well.
2. Peel and stone the peaches, chop into 0.5 cm dice and measure 1 cupful. Alternatively, drain the canned peach slices and prepare as above.
3. Combine the golden syrup and melted butter. Beat in the milk and egg.
4. Alternately fold in the diced peaches and egg mixture with the dry ingredients until just combined.
5. Fill 12 greased muffin tins with the mixture. Mix the crystallized ginger and raw sugar together, and sprinkle a little over each muffin.
6. Bake at 200°C for 15-18 minutes or until well risen and golden. Cool on a wire rack.

Variations:
Use apricots, pears or feijoas instead of peaches.

Javanese-spiced muffins

12 muffins

2 cups self rising flour
¼ cup cornflour
½ tsp baking powder
½ tsp each of ground nutmeg,
   cloves and cinnamon
2 slices canned pineapple

75 grams butter
2 eggs
½ cup milk
¼ cup coconut milk
2 tblsp pineapple juice

1. Sift the flour, cornflour, baking powder, nutmeg, cloves and cinnamon into a bowl and make a well in the centre. Finely chop the pineapple slices.
2. Melt the butter and mix together with the eggs, milk, coconut milk and pineapple juice.
3. Pour the liquid mixture into the well in the dry ingredients. Add the chopped pineapple and fold together with a holed spoon. Do not over mix.
4. Fill 12 greased muffin tins with the mixture.
5. Bake at 210°C for 15 minutes until golden and cooked.
6. Serve warm with butter.

Chocolate-chip muffins

12 muffins

Buttery and just plain yumptious, chocolate-chip muffins will be a great success with family members of all ages.

2 cups flour
4 tsp baking powder
pinch salt
100 grams butter
¾ cup caster sugar

2 eggs
½ tsp vanilla essence
½ cup chocolate chips
1 cup milk

1. Sift the flour, baking powder and salt into a large bowl.
2. Put the butter, sugar, eggs and vanilla essence into a food processor and process until light and well mixed.
3. Add the chocolate chips and pulse to mix.
4. Fold the chocolate-chip mixture and the milk into the dry ingredients, using a holed spoon, until just mixed.
5. Fill 12 greased muffin tins with the mixture.
6. Bake at 220°C for 12-15 minutes or until cooked. Serve warm.

Variations:
*   Add the grated rind of one orange to the creamed mixture for jaffa muffins.
*   Add half a cup of chopped walnuts or pecans.

Cook's Tip:

Use small chips, not chocolate drops. If you only have drop-style chocolate bits on hand, pulse in a processor to chop finely before adding to recipe.

Coconut and orange muffins

12 muffins

These are lovely muffins, delicately flavoured with coconut cream and a little extra sweet flavour from the orange rind.

2 eggs
¾ cup caster sugar
125 grams butter
grated rind 1 orange

2½ cups flour
5 tsp baking powder
1 cup coconut milk
¼ cup coconut shreds

1. Put the eggs and sugar into a food processor and process until well blended. Add the butter and orange rind and process until creamy.
2. Sift flour and baking powder into a large bowl and make a well in the centre.
3. Add the creamed mixture and fold into the dry ingredients with the coconut milk.
4. Fill 12 greased muffin tins with the mixture. Top each with a few shreds of coconut.
5. Bake at 200°C for 15 minutes or until well risen and golden.

Cook's Tips:

After grating an orange or lemon on a grater, remove the rind using a glazing brush. Trying to get the last morsels of zest from a grater without one is beyond frustration. Don't forget to use self rising flour where the ratio of flour to baking powder is 1 cup to 1 teaspoon.

Blueberry yoghurt muffins

12 muffins

Why not try raspberries for a change.

Blueberry muffins are an all-time favourite with New Zealanders, having come to us from the United States. This variation uses a fruit yoghurt to add extra flavour.

2½ cups flour
1½ tsp baking powder
1 tsp baking soda
½ cup melted butter
1 egg

½ cup water
200-gram tub boysenberry yoghurt
2 cups defrosted (but not hot) blueberries

1. Sift the flour, baking powder and baking soda into a large bowl and make a well in the centre.
2. Mix the butter, egg, water and boysenberry yoghurt together.
3. Pour the liquid ingredients into the well in the dry ingredients. Add the blueberries.
4. Mix with a holed spoon only until all ingredients are incorporated. Do not over mix.
5. Fill 12 greased muffin tins with the mixture.
6. Bake at 200°C for approximately 12-15 minutes until well risen, golden and cooked. Serve warm and well buttered.

Best-ever banana muffins

12 muffins

These are more like mini cakes than muffins in texture. The recipe comes from the most wonderful next-door neighbour that anybody could ever wish to have. Jan is a mine of wonderful recipes from years back. Any new idea that Jan passes on to me, I enjoy very much; it is usually well tried and tested in her house before it makes its way to mine, thanks to her children and grandchildren.

3 small or 2 medium-sized bananas
¾ cup caster sugar
1 egg
2 cups flour

1 tsp baking soda
1½ tsp baking powder
½ tsp salt
½ cup melted butter

1. Mash the bananas well.
2. Mix in the caster sugar and egg.
3. Sift together the flour, baking soda, baking powder and salt and sprinkle evenly over the top of the banana mixture.
4. Carefully stir the ingredients together with the melted butter.
5. Fill 12 greased muffin tins with the mixture.
6. Bake at 200°C for 12-15 minutes until well risen, golden and cooked.
7. Serve warm with butter.

Cook's Tip:

Blackened bananas are wonderful for cooking with. They can be frozen if you have an over supply at any one time. Put them into the freezer whole; take them out and use as required.

Yoghurt adds lightness as well as taste to these quick-to-prepare muffins.

1 orange
1 egg
½ cup caster sugar
½ cup chopped dates or sultanas
½ cup melted butter
2 cups flour

1 tsp baking soda
1 tsp baking powder
2 tblsp wheatgerm or oat bran
200-gram tub apricot yoghurt
½ cup milk
12 walnut halves

Orange and date muffins

12 muffins

1. Grate the rind from the orange. Peel away the white orange pith that remains with a knife and discard. Chop the orange flesh. Put the orange, orange rind, egg and sugar into a food processor and process for 2 minutes.
2. Pulse in the chopped dates or sultanas and melted butter.
3. Sift together the flour, baking soda, baking powder and wheatgerm or oat bran and sprinkle evenly over the top of the liquid ingredients in the food processor. On top of the flour spread over the apricot yoghurt and milk.
4. Pulse only until all ingredients are mixed.
5. Fill 12 well greased muffin tins with the mixture and decorate with a walnut half.
6. Bake at 200°C for 15-18 minutes, until golden brown and well cooked. Serve warm.

I designed this recipe for New Zealand cheese and we cooked it in large Texas muffin containers. These are absolutely delicious topped with tomato and herbs, drizzled with a little olive oil. Great for accompanying a lunch menu on the weekend.

2 cups self rising flour
½ tsp salt
1 tsp ground black pepper
2 tsp paprika
2 tblsp each of chopped fresh thyme
  and oregano (or 1 tsp each dried)

½ tsp cayenne pepper
50 grams butter
2 cups grated tasty cheese
1 egg
1¾ cups milk

Creole cheese muffins

12 muffins

1. Sift flour, salt, pepper, paprika, fresh herbs and cayenne into a bowl. Rub in the butter until the mixture resembles crumbs. Stir in 1½ cups of the grated cheese and make a well in the centre.
2. Beat the egg and milk together and stir into the dry ingredients. Mix with a holed spoon to make a smooth batter. Do not over mix or the muffins will peak.
3. Fill 12 greased muffin tins with mixture. Sprinkle the remaining ½ cup of cheese evenly on top.
4. Bake at 200°C for 12-15 minutes until golden brown and cooked.

Keep grated cheese in the freezer. It keeps well and you can break off how ever much you need at any time.

BAKING
WITH
YEAST

Cook's Tip:

It's hard to tell when a dough has proven to twice its size. When the dough is placed in the loaf tin for the second rising, allow it to prove until the dough reaches the top of the sides of the tin.

In all my years of cooking, one of the most satisfying areas has been baking with yeast. There is nothing quite so wonderful as the smell of freshly baked bread hot from the oven, served warm with lashings of butter.

Like any other area of cookery, and baking in particular, there are guidelines to ensure a successful end result. However, most mistakes can be corrected.

Baking bread is no longer the chore we once thought it to be with food processors to help. The recipes in this chapter have all at one time been made in the food processor, cutting back time and elbow grease. I rarely make bread by hand. I have a Cuisinart food processor, which has a motor with sufficient grunt to make a kilogram of flour into bread. It is truly wonderful.

Learn the basic bread recipe first and branch out from there. I have many favourites in this chapter. Right now in my home, focaccia (with numerous variations) is the most popular and it's also a great first recipe to begin with.

Cook's Tip:

Kneading the dough is a very important stage. It is necessary to evenly distribute the yeast cells and promote elasticity. The dough must become smooth and shiny; this takes 10-15 minutes by hand.

Opposite (from top to bottom): Frangipani Cake (page 77), Kevi Gingerbread (page 78), Marseilles Cake (page 90).

This looks spectacular and is just wonderful sliced and served with coffee. I made the recipe twice, making the dough in the food processor on one occasion. The dough was not as good, so I'd recommend doing it all by hand for the best results if you have time.

Poppy seed roll

1 cup milk
½ cup water
1 tblsp sugar
1 tblsp butter
4 tsp dried yeast or 3 tblsp Surebake
4 egg yolks

100 grams butter
1 cup sugar
5-5½ cups high grade flour
1 tsp salt
milk to glaze

Filling

½ cup sultanas
4 × 40-gram pkt poppy seeds
¼ cup milk

¼ cup honey
grated rind of one lemon

Pretty opium poppies are the source of poppy seeds as well as the highly narcotic drug. The poppy seeds are harmless in cooking and it takes 1000 seeds to make 5 grams in weight! Crush them to release their flavour.

1. Put the milk, water, first measure of sugar and butter into a small saucepan and warm to blood heat. Remove from the heat and stir in the dried yeast. Set aside for 15 minutes until the mixture is frothy.
2. Beat together the egg yolks, second measure of butter and sugar.
3. Sift 5 cups of the flour and salt into a large bowl and make a well in the centre.
4. Add the frothy mixture and the creamed mixture to the flour and mix quickly to form a soft dough. If the dough is a bit sticky add the remaining flour. Then turn out onto a floured board and knead well for 10 minutes until the dough is smooth.
5. Turn the dough over in a greased bowl and cover with greased plastic wrap. Set aside in a warm place to rise until the dough is double in bulk. Usually this takes about an hour, depending on the temperature (of the day) it may take a little more or a little less.
6. Roll the dough out to form a 60 cm × 60 cm square. Spread the filling over the dough leaving a 1 cm border all the way around.
7. Roll the dough up from one side only to the centre. Roll the other side up to the centre. Brush the centre with a little milk and the dough will stay together. Transfer the dough to a greased baking tray and cover with a clean towel. Leave in a warm place to rise until doubled in size.
8. Brush the top with milk. Bake at 190°C for 40-45 minutes or until the dough sounds hollow when tapped from underneath. Transfer to a cake rack to cool.

Filling

In a small saucepan, put the sultanas, poppy seeds, milk, honey and the lemon rind. Simmer for 5 minutes. Pulse 3-4 times in the processor to crack some of the seeds.

Cook's Tip:

Sponging the yeast means to dissolve the yeast in liquid, allowing it to froth up so that the yeast is working. Allow it to froth up well. If the yeast does not sponge it is dead.

Cook's Tip:

To judge whether you have kneaded the dough enough, press your finger into the dough; if the dough springs back, it is kneaded sufficiently. If it does not, there is more work to do!

Opposite: Ginger Pear Pinwheels (*at back*) (page 100), Basic Scones with jam (*left*) (page 100), Wholemeal Date Scones (page 101).

Dutch poppy seed buns

8 buns

These buns are enriched with milk powder and literally covered with poppy seeds.

½ cup warm water
3 tsp dried yeast or 2 tblsp Surebake
1 tblsp sugar
3½ cups high grade flour

¼ cup milk powder
1 tsp salt
1 cup cold water
2 × 40-gram pkt poppy seeds

Egg glaze
1 egg
½ teaspoon salt

1. Put the warm water in a large jug and sprinkle over the yeast and sugar. Stir well. Set aside for 10-12 minutes until frothy.
2. Put the flour, milk powder and salt into a food processor and pulse 3 or 4 times to sift.
3. Add the cold water to the frothed yeast.
4. With the motor running, pour the liquid down the feed tube until the dough cleans the inside of the food processor bowl. Have a little extra water at hand if needed. The dough should be quite firm.
5. Process for 1 minute to knead the dough.
6. Turn the dough over in a greased bowl. Cover with greased plastic wrap and set aside in a warm place for 1-1½ hours, or until double in bulk.
7. Knock dough back and turn onto a lightly floured surface. Divide into 8 equal portions.
8. Roll each portion into a ball and cover. Leave to rise for 8-10 minutes.
9. Put the poppy seeds onto a saucer. Brush the top of each bun with the egg glaze and dip into the poppy seeds.
10. Place the buns on a greased baking tray and leave uncovered to rise for a further 15 minutes.
11. Bake at 200°C for 12-15 minutes or until lightly browned.
12. Buns are cooked when they are tapped underneath and sound hollow. Cool on a cake rack. These buns freeze well. Freeze them while still warm. Serve warm.

Egg glaze
Beat egg and salt together.

By hand
Sponge the yeast as for step 1. Sift the dry ingredients into a bowl and make a well in the centre. Stir the water into the frothy liquid and then pour into the centre, mixing well to form a dough. Once the flour has incorporated the liquid, turn out onto a floured board and knead well for 10 minutes until the dough is smooth. Continue from step 6.

Variation:
Substitute sesame seeds for poppy seeds.

½ cup warm water
pinch sugar
2½ tsp dried yeast or 2 tblsp Surebake
2 cups water at room temperature

¼ cup good olive oil
1 kg high grade flour
1 tblsp sea salt
½ cup extra warm water

Focaccia

1. Mix the ½ cup water and pinch of sugar together in a small bowl. Stir in the yeast and set aside in a warm place for 10-15 minutes or until frothy.
2. Stir the frothed mixture into the 2 cups of water and olive oil.
3. Put the flour and salt into a food processor and pulse to sift.
4. Have the frothed liquid and extra water at hand. With the machine running, pour the frothed liquid down the feed tube as fast as the flour can absorb it. Add sufficient extra water to produce a soft dough.
5. After the dough gathers into a mass, process it for a further 20 seconds. Turn onto a floured board and knead for 2-3 minutes.
6. Place the dough in a lightly oiled bowl and cover with oiled plastic wrap.
7. Set aside for 1-1½ hours or until double in bulk.
8. Divide dough into 3 equal portions.
9. Roll each portion out to a 20 cm round, and place on a greased baking tray.
10. Cover with a teatowel and set aside in a warm place for 30 minutes. Dimple the dough with your fingers.
11. Cover again with the teatowel and leave in a warm place for 1 hour until double in bulk.
12. Brush liberally with olive oil and sprinkle extra sea salt over the top.
13. Bake at 200°C for 20-25 minutes. If possible, spray with water 3 times during the first 10 minutes of cooking to give a golden crusty top. Serve warm.

By hand

Mix the ½ cup of water and pinch of sugar together in a small bowl. Sprinkle the yeast over and set aside in a warm place for 10 minutes or until frothy. Stir the frothed mixture into the 2 cups of warm water and olive oil. Transfer to a large bowl. Sift the flour and salt together. Add two cups of flour to the water and whisk until smooth. Stir in the remaining flour one cup at a time until the dough comes together. Turn onto a floured bench and knead for ten minutes until smooth and velvety. Continue from step 6.

Variations:
- Add ½ cup chopped olives to the dough when processing.
- Stud the top of each round with sprigs of fresh rosemary, olives or sliced dried tomatoes.

Cook's Tip:

The microwave can be used for the first proving. Place the dough in a greased microwave-proof bowl and cover with greased plastic wrap. Stand for 10 minutes, then microwave on 10% for 10 minutes. Stand for a further 10 minutes and repeat the microwave process until the dough has doubled in bulk.

Basic white bread

1½ tsp dried yeast or 1½ tblsp Surebake
1¼ cups warm water or milk
1 tsp sugar
3 cups pure flour or high grade flour

2 tblsp soft butter
½-1 tsp salt
1-3 tblsp extra water

1. Mix together the yeast, warm water or milk and sugar and set aside for 15 minutes until frothy.
2. Put the flour, butter and salt into a food processor and process until the butter is well mixed in.
3. With the motor running, pour the frothy yeast liquid down the feed tube.
4. Add an extra 1-3 tablespoons of water to make a soft dough. Process the dough for 1 minute.
5. Transfer to a greased bowl and cover with greased plastic wrap. Set aside in a warm place for about 1 hour or until double in bulk.
6. Knock down dough and shape into a loaf. Place in a greased 8 cm × 20 cm loaf tin. Cover with greased plastic wrap and set aside for 30-40 minutes, until the dough doubles in size.
7. Brush with milk and sprinkle with poppy seeds, sesame seeds, linseeds or even a good dusting of flour.
8. Bake at 220°C for 30 minutes. When the loaf is cooked it sounds hollow when tapped underneath. Cool on a cake rack.

By hand

To make the dough by hand, prove the yeast following step 1. Then rub the butter into the flour and mix the liquid and flour in a bowl. Then knead on a floured board for 10 minutes until the dough is smooth. Continue from step 5.

Cook's Tip:

If you want to make two loaves, do not double the yeast quantity — 2½ teaspoons will be sufficient.

Cook's Tip:

Knocking back or punching down means to punch down the dough once it is well risen from the first rising. This eliminates any large air holes and ensures an even-textured bread when cooked.

Serve this warm, thickly sliced with salads and salamis, or toasted and drizzled with a little olive oil.

Olive and onion bread

½ cup warm water
1 tsp sugar
1 tblsp dried yeast or 3 tblsp Surebake

4 cups high grade flour
1 cup warm water
¼ cup olive oil

Filling
2 onions
1 clove garlic
2 tblsp olive oil
¼ cup chopped olives

1 tblsp chopped fresh rosemary (or 1 tsp dried)
pepper to taste

To glaze
extra olive oil
rock salt

1. Mix the ½ cup of warm water, sugar and yeast together and set aside for about 10 minutes until frothy.
2. Put the flour in a food processor and pulse to sift. With the motor running, pour the yeast liquid and extra cup of water and olive oil down the feed tube to make a soft dough. Process the dough for 1 minute.
3. Put into a greased bowl and cover with greased plastic wrap. Set aside in a warm place for about 50 minutes until about double in bulk.
4. Knock back and roll dough out to a round about 3 cm thick. Spread the filling over half the dough and roll the other half of the dough on top. Press edges together firmly.
5. Place on a greased tray, cover with a cloth and leave for a further 20 minutes.
6. Brush with olive oil and dust with rock salt. Bake at 220°C for 10 minutes then reduce to 200°C for a further 15 minutes.

Filling
Peel the onions and garlic. Slice finely. Heat the olive oil in a frying pan and cook the onion and garlic over a low heat until soft but not coloured. Add the olives, rosemary and pepper.

By hand
Sponge the yeast in the liquid as in step 1. Sift the flour into a large bowl and make a well in the centre. Gradually pour in the frothy yeast mixture, mixing to form a soft dough. When almost all the flour has been absorbed, turn the dough out and knead well for 10 minutes on a lightly floured board until smooth. Continue from step 3.

Cook's Tip:

When I prove dough without a microwave, I wrap the bowl in a blanket and place in a warm room. I prefer this method.

Vary the flavour of the bread with the olives you use.
Manzanilla are plain green olives from Spain.
Use stuffed or plain green.
Mission olives are round fat black olives from Greece or Spain.
Kalamata are olives with a mild but rich flavour from Greece.

Ann's coffee cake

This recipe is from girlfriend and colleague Ann Boardman, who lives in paradise in South Auckland on a 10-acre property with horses and a few cows. Ann prepared this at a champagne brunch one summer Sunday morning. It is quick and delicious. You can vary the flavour of the cake by using different nuts such as hazelnuts or pecans.

¼ cup sugar	2 tsp dried yeast or 1½ tblsp Surebake
½ tsp salt	1¾ cups high grade flour
50 grams butter	1 egg
½ cup boiling water	

Topping

25 grams butter	½ cup chopped walnuts
¼ cup brown sugar	2 tblsp chopped crystallized ginger
¼ cup fresh white breadcrumbs	

Cook's Tip:

American recipes often call for 1 package of dried yeast. This converts to 1 scant tablespoon dried yeast or approximately 3 tablespoons Surebake.

1. In a bowl put the sugar, salt and butter. Pour over the boiling water and stir to dissolve the sugar. Stand 5 minutes then stir in the yeast. Stand for 10-15 minutes until the mixture is frothy.
2. Sift the flour and beat half of it into the liquid. Beat the egg and add along with the remaining flour. The dough will be fairly sticky.
3. Spread into a greased 23 cm round tin. Scatter topping over the dough and set in a warm place for about 40 minutes or until double in bulk.
4. Bake at 190°C for about 35 minutes or until cooked. Serve warm.

Topping

Melt butter, stir in the sugar, breadcrumbs, walnuts and ginger, and mix well.

Cornbread

This Yankee Doodle quick bread makes a change as an accompaniment to soups or casseroles. Unlike the other breads in this section, it does not contain yeast.

1½ cups pure flour	1 tsp salt
½ cup fine cornmeal	1½ cups milk
½ cup sugar	¼ cup melted butter
½ cup cornflour	1 egg
1 tblsp baking powder	

1. Sift the flour, cornmeal, sugar, cornflour, baking powder and salt into a large bowl and make a well in the centre.
2. In a separate bowl combine the milk, butter and egg.
3. Stir the liquid ingredients into the dry ingredients, blending with a holed spoon only until just mixed — do not overbeat.

4. Pour the mixture into a greased, floured and lined 20 cm square cake tin.
5. Bake at 180°C for 50 minutes until a cake skewer inserted comes out clean. Serve warm.

Variations:
- Bake the cornbread in a cast-iron pan; serve it from the pan.
- Add chopped, cooked bacon and spring onion to the batter.
- Add ¼ cup of grated Parmesan cheese and ¼ cup chopped fresh oregano to the batter.

Cook's Tips:

If you over beat the batter, the cornbread will peak like Mt Everest during cooking.
You may not like to add salt, but you really do need it or your cornbread will be tasteless.

Lynne's beer bread

I have two wonderful friends, Greg and Lynne, who are great at entertaining, especially come the summer barbecue season when Lynne serves this quick and easy to make bread. It couldn't be easier — in fact it's fail proof — made with beer.

1½ cup self rising flour
1 cup self rising wholemeal flour
½ tsp salt
355-ml can beer

Toppings
¼ cup of oats, linseeds, pumpkin seeds or sunflower seeds

1. Mix the flours and salt together in a bowl and make a well in the centre.
2. Using a wooden spoon, stir the beer into the flour. Beat well with the wooden spoon.
3. Transfer the batter to a well greased and floured 20 cm × 10 cm loaf tin. Sprinkle over one of the toppings.
4. Bake at 180°C for about 50-60 minutes or until the loaf sounds hollow when tapped underneath. Cool on a cake rack.

Cook's Tip:

Vary the flavour of the bread with different beers. I use standard strength beer.

Stollen

Stollen, or Christstollen as it is really called, is German Christmas Cake. The marzipan centre represents Christ; the cake, the blanket He was wrapped in. Stollen is always made in my home at Christmas.

1 cup sultanas and currants
2 tblsp brandy
3 cups high grade flour
pinch salt
3 tblsp caster sugar
¼ cup mixed peel
¼ cup sliced almonds
¼ cup finely chopped pawpaw
   (or use mixed peel)
1 cup milk

1 tsp caster sugar
2 tsp dried yeast or 2 tblsp Surebake
1 egg
75 grams melted butter
1 tblsp softened butter
200 grams marzipan
rosewater to flavour
50 grams extra melted butter for
   brushing
½ cup icing sugar for dusting

Each year I make up several Stollen. Then dusted heavily with icing sugar and tied with ribbon I send them off to close friends as a Christmas gift. It's almost a tradition now and one we all get to enjoy.

1. Toss the sultanas and currants in the brandy and set aside for 1-2 hours.
2. Sift the flour and salt together. Take 1 cup of flour and set aside. To the remaining 2 cups of flour, add the 3 tablespoons caster sugar, mixed peel, almonds, pawpaw, sultanas and currants. Set aside.
3. Bring the milk to blood heat with the 1 teaspoon sugar. Stir in the dried yeast and set aside for 10 minutes, or until the mixture is frothy.
4. Pour the yeasty liquid into the bowl containing the 1 cup of flour. Add the egg and melted butter and beat well to achieve a smooth batter. Stand, covered, in a warm place until the batter has doubled in bulk and is bubbly. Stir this mixture into the flour and fruit mixture. Turn out onto a floured board and knead for about 10 minutes, until smooth.
5. Turn dough over in a greased bowl and spread over the softened butter. Cover with plastic wrap and set aside in a warm place for 1 hour or until double in bulk.
6. Knock dough down and roll it out to a large oval, about 1½ cm thick.
7. Knead the marzipan with a little rosewater to flavour. Roll the marzipan out to form a thick sausage the length of the dough and place it right of centre. Brush the edge of the dough with milk. Roll the dough over the marzipan and press the edges together firmly. Transfer to a greased baking tray. Cover with a clean towel and set aside in a warm place for about 40 minutes until the dough has doubled in bulk.
8. Bake at 200°C for 10 minutes, then lower the oven to 180°C for a further 35-40 minutes. The dough is cooked if it sounds hollow when tapped underneath. Transfer the Stollen out onto a cake rack to cool.
9. Brush well with the extra butter and cover liberally with sifted icing sugar. Serve cut in slices.

Opposite (from top to bottom): Blueberry Yoghurt Muffins (page 110), Best-ever Banana Muffins (page 110), Best-ever Bran and Honey Muffins (page 106).

Following page: Hot Cross Buns (page 132).

Cook's Tip:

This is wonderful toasted and buttered!

1 tsp sugar
2 tsp dried yeast or 2 tblsp Surebake
1¼ cup milk, warm
3½ cups high grade flour
75 grams softened butter

½ tsp salt
2 eggs
½ cup vanilla sugar or caster sugar
50 grams softened butter
icing sugar

Dutch Easter bread

Filling

¾ cup ground almonds
¼ cup sugar
½ cup sultanas

¼ cup finely chopped cherries
extra milk for glazing

1. Sprinkle sugar and yeast into the milk and leave for 15 minutes or until slightly frothy. Add milk mixture to 1 cup flour, and stand for a further 5 minutes in a warm place until the batter is frothy again.
2. Put the first measure of butter into a food processor with the flour and salt and process until it resembles crumbs.
3. Separate the eggs, then add the egg yolks to the frothed yeast mixture.
4. Pour all the frothed yeast mixture into the processor and process to a soft dough, adding more milk if necessary.
5. Turn the dough over in a greased bowl. Cover with plastic wrap and place in a warm place for an hour or until double in bulk.
6. Turn the dough out and punch down. Roll out to an oblong 1½ cm thick.
7. Spread the second measure of butter over the dough then carefully spread over the filling.
8. Roll up, ensuring the join is on the bottom and the ends are tucked in.
9. Place the loaf on a greased baking tray. Cover with a clean towel, and leave in a warm place for 45 minutes or until double in bulk.
10. Glaze with a little milk.
11. Bake at 190°C for about 45 minutes, or until the loaf sounds hollow when tapped underneath.
12. Cool on a cake rack. To serve, sift icing sugar over the loaf and slice thickly.

Filling

Whip the egg whites with a fork until broken down. Mix in the almonds, sugar, sultanas and cherries.

By hand

Sponge the yeast as outlined in step 1. Sift the flour and salt into a large bowl and rub in the first measure of butter. Make a well in the centre. Add the egg yolks to the frothy yeast mixture and begin to mix into the flour. Once almost all the flour has been absorbed, turn the dough out onto a lightly floured board and knead well for 10 minutes until the dough is smooth. Continue from step 5.

Cook's Tip:

For a wholemeal bread use half plain and half wholemeal flour.

Preceding page (anticlockwise from top left): Irish Soda Bread (page 123), Dutch Poppy Seed Buns (page 114), Pumpkin and Basil Bread (page 125), Focaccia (page 115), Basic White Bread (page 116).
Opposite: Mini Christmas Cakes (page 96), Stollen (page 120).

Glenda's fruit plait

This fruit plait was created especially for *Next* by one of my colleagues and guest cook, Glenda Gourley. Glenda, John and son Benjamin enjoy this fresh or toasted.

¼ cup warm water
¼ tsp sugar
1½ tsp dried yeast or 1½ tblsp Surebake
3 cups high grade flour
1 cup wholemeal flour
2 tsp sugar
1 tsp salt
½ cup milk
½ cup hot water

2 tblsp melted butter
2 large apples
1 cup apricots roughly chopped
1 cup prunes roughly chopped
1 cup raw sugar
1 cup water
2 tsp mixed spice
milk to glaze

1. Put the first measure of warm water in a small bowl. The water should be tepid. Stir in the first measure of sugar and sprinkle with the yeast. Stir. Stand in a warm place until the mixture becomes frothy. Give the yeast at least 10 minutes to return to active life.
2. Put the flour, wholemeal flour, second measure of sugar and salt into a food processor and pulse to sift.
3. With the motor running, pour the milk, hot water, melted butter and frothy yeast mixture down the feed tube to form a soft dough. Process for 1 minute.
4. Place the dough into a greased bowl, turn over to grease the top. Cover with greased plastic wrap and stand in a warm place until doubled in size. The dough will take about 1 hour to double in bulk.
5. Grate the apples, do not peel. Place the apples, apricots, prunes, raw sugar, water and mixed spice in a saucepan. Cover and simmer for 10-15 minutes, stirring frequently until the mixture resembles a thick paste. Watch that it doesn't catch.
6. Remove the dough from the bowl and punch down.
7. Turn onto a lightly floured bench and roll the dough into a rectangle 30 cm × 40 cm. Mark into thirds length-wise. Cut slashes on an angle at 3 cm spacing down the length of the outer thirds. Take care that these are the same on both sides.
8. Spread the fruit filling along the centre third. Overlap the side strips across the filling. Transfer onto a greased baking tray. Cover with greased plastic wrap and stand in a warm place for 30-40 minutes until doubled in size.
9. Remove the plastic wrap and glaze with milk. Bake at 180°C for 30-40 minutes or until golden brown. The loaf is cooked if it sounds hollow when tapped underneath. Cool on a cake rack.

By hand

Sponge the yeast as outlined in step 1. Sift the flours and salt into a large bowl and stir through the sugar. Make a well in the centre. Gradually mix in the milk, hot water, melted butter and yeast mixture. Once most of the

Cook's Tip:

Unless the weather is very cold, you don't need to find a special warm place to leave dough to rise, as the dough will generate its own warmth as the yeast works. The warmth of the kitchen or a sunroom should be sufficient.

flour has been absorbed, turn the dough out onto a lightly floured board and knead well for 10 minutes until smooth. Continue from step 4.

Variation:
Use another fruit combination, such as dates and peaches, or mixed dried fruit. The bread lasts well kept in an airtight container, and you can reheat slices in the microwave (10-15 seconds on high).

Cook's Tip:

To knead, push the dough down firmly with the heel of the hand and push the dough away from you. Lift the edge of the dough with your fingers and bring into the centre. Give the dough a quarter turn and repeat. Continue this way until the dough is smooth and slightly shiny when rubbed. It should be elastic and spring back when pressed with your finger. Don't use too much flour as you knead. The second kneading, punching down and kneading process, or 'knocking back' as it is often called, redistributes the gas bubbles produced by the yeast, helps the gluten to develop and reactivates the yeast so that it will renew its work and form new air balloons. This second kneading should be gentle and is done to help shape the dough for cooking.

Irish soda bread

Soda breads are easy to make and require very little effort to achieve an excellent result. Covering the bread with a cake tin for the first part of cooking will give an even-shaped loaf and it will also help keep the bread moist.

3½ cups high grade flour
2 tsp baking soda
2 tsp cream of tartar
½ tsp salt

50 grams butter
1½-2 cups buttermilk
¼ cup extra flour

1. Sift the flour, baking soda, cream of tartar and salt into a bowl.
2. Rub in the butter well. Make a well in the centre.
3. Using a wooden spoon, add sufficient buttermilk to mix to a soft dough.
4. Turn out onto a floured board and knead very lightly.
5. Mould the bread into a 20 cm round and place on a well greased and floured baking tray.
6. Make a cross in the centre and dust the top with extra flour.
7. Cover the bread with a greased 23 cm round cake tin.
8. Bake at 200°C for 40 minutes, removing the baking tin 15 minutes into cooking time. Tap the bread underneath and if it is cooked it will sound hollow.
9. Cool on a cake rack. Serve fresh, or toast when 1-2 days old.

For a real earthy Soda Bread make it with ¾ wholemeal flour and ¼ plain — you can also jazz it up by adding seeds such as pumpkin, linseed, sunflower, sesame or poppy!

Cook's Tip:

If you do not have buttermilk, use 2 cups of milk and sour it with 1 tblsp of lemon juice. Allow to stand for 10 minutes.

Savarin

Serves 12

Flavour the syrup with rosewater or orange blossom and garnish with buds of miniature roses or orange blossoms.

Cook's Tips:

A savarin tin is a plain ring mould with a rounded base. If you do not have one, use a similar size ring tin. If you use a loose-bottomed tin remove the cake to a large bowl to pour the syrup over, otherwise it will run out at the join.

Beating the mixture by hand may seem odd but in reality it produces an excellent finished product. A food processor will get clogged up under the blade and stop. A wooden spoon tends to not be able to take the pressure. Use only one hand and keep the other clean for grabbing at things.

If you do not have kirsch, do not panic. I use whatever I seem to have on hand. If you are using berry fruits, maybe try a berry liqueur. If using apricots or peaches, try an orange liqueur. Lemon juice is very nice in place of alcohol.

Savarin is a buttery, rich yeast ring, smothered in a kirsch-flavoured syrup and served piled with fresh fruit and cream. Traditionally it is made by a double rising of the batter; I make this one-rise recipe, which takes no time at all and gives a very good result.

2 cups high grade flour	1 tsp dried yeast or 1 tblsp Surebake
1 tsp salt	4 eggs
¾ cup warm milk	½ cup cooled melted butter
1 tblsp sugar	

Syrup
2 cups caster sugar
2¼ cups water
1 vanilla pod or 1 tsp vanilla essence
½ cup kirsch, other favourite liqueur or fruit juice

Filling
2 punnets fresh berries
300-ml bottle cream
icing sugar to sweeten

1. Sift the flour and salt into a large bowl.
2. Warm the milk to blood heat. Stir in the sugar and yeast and set aside for 10-15 minutes or until it is very frothy.
3. Make a well in the centre of the flour and add the yeast mixture and the eggs.
4. Use your hands to blend the ingredients into a batter and then continue to beat the dough with your hands until the batter is shiny. This will take about 10 minutes.
5. Add the butter and beat a further 3 minutes. Sit the bowl on its side on a bench to make sure you can really beat the batter.
6. Pour the batter into a well greased and floured 23 cm savarin tin.
7. Set aside in a warm place for about 1 hour until the batter has doubled in bulk.
8. Bake at 190°C for about 25 minutes until the dough is cooked.
9. Remove from the oven and allow to stand for 5 minutes.
10. Loosen the cake from the tin and then pour half the syrup over the cake. Stand 10 minutes and repeat.
11. Invert the cooled syrup-saturated cake onto a cake plate to serve. Fill the centre with whipped sweetened cream and fresh berries.

Syrup
Put the sugar, water and vanilla pod or essence into a saucepan and bring to the boil, stirring until the sugar has dissolved. Simmer 5 minutes. Remove the vanilla pod if using and stir in the kirsch, liqueur or fruit juice.

Pumpkin and basil bread

It was a cold Auckland Saturday the first day I made this bread. A friend, Simon, and his daughter, Alice, who was then 1½, called to see me on their weekly dad and daughter walk. Freshly baked and served with plenty of salad, all three of us had a great meal; some was even taken home for Mum, Anna. When no longer fresh, this is delicious toasted and served with thin slices of ham and mustard pickles.

1½ tsp dried yeast or 1½ tblsp Surebake
½ cup warm water
pinch sugar
3½ cups high grade flour
1 tsp salt

50 grams butter
6 leaves fresh basil or 1 tblsp dried
1 cup mashed pumpkin★
milk to glaze
¼ cup pumpkin seeds

1. Sprinkle the dried yeast over the warm water in a bowl and stir in the sugar. Set the mixture aside for 15 minutes or until it is very frothy.
2. Put the flour, salt, butter and basil into a food processor fitted with the metal blade and process until well incorporated.
3. Mix the frothy yeast mixture and pumpkin together and add to the food processor. Process the mixture for 1 minute. The dough mixture should be very soft. Add more water if necessary.
4. Turn the dough out onto a floured board and bring together. Place in a large greased bowl and cover with greased plastic wrap. Set aside in a warm place for 60 minutes or until the dough has doubled in bulk.
5. Turn out the dough, and shape into a loaf. Place in a greased 20 cm × 10 cm loaf tin. Cover with greased plastic wrap again and leave in a warm place until the dough reaches the top of the tin. Brush with milk to glaze and sprinkle the pumpkin seeds over the top.
6. Bake at 200°C for 35-40 minutes or until the loaf sounds hollow when tapped underneath. Cool on a cake rack.

★ The pumpkin must be dry, not wet, as this will affect the amount of liquid required.

By hand
Sponge the yeast as outlined in step 1. Sift the flour and salt into a large bowl. Rub in the butter until the mixture resembles fine crumbs. Stir through the finely chopped basil and make a well in the centre. Mix the pumpkin with the frothy yeast mixture and mix into the flour. Once almost all the liquid has been incorporated, turn the mixture out onto a lightly floured board and knead well for 10 minutes until the dough is smooth. Continue from step 4.

Variation:
Make the dough with 1 cup of wholemeal flour and 2½ cups of plain.

Cook's Tip:

Make the dough into three even balls and place each ball into the greased tin so that you have a traditional old-style loaf and you can tear each section apart. To get the portions even-sized weigh the dough then divide and weigh. Do this also when dividing dough up for bread rolls.

Citrus raisin loaf

Not too sweet and not too raisin-y, this loaf flavoured with lemon rind is wonderful fresh or toasted and served with lemon butter when it is a little older.

2 tsp dried yeast or 2 tblsp Surebake
¾ cup milk
pinch sugar
1 egg
3 cups high grade flour
1 tsp salt

2 tblsp brown sugar
grated rind 1 lemon
50 grams butter
1 cup raisins
milk to glaze

Topping
25 grams butter
¼ cup icing sugar

Cook's Tip:

When you take a loaf from the oven, remove it from the tin after 3-4 minutes so that it does not sweat. If the loaf is soft around the edges when removed from the cake tin, return it to the oven for about 3-4 minutes to crisp the outside.

1. Sprinkle the dried yeast over the warm milk in a bowl and stir in the sugar. Set the mixture aside for 15 minutes or until frothy. Beat in the egg.
2. Put the flour, salt, sugar, lemon rind and butter into a food processor and process for 1 minute.
3. With the motor running, pour the frothy yeast mixture down the feed tube and process to form a soft dough. If the dough looks too dry, add a little more milk. Process 1 minute. Pulse in the raisins.
4. Turn the dough out onto a floured board and bring together. Turn dough into a greased bowl and cover with greased plastic wrap. Set aside in a warm place for 1 hour or until double in bulk.
5. Turn the dough out and shape into a loaf. Place in a greased 20 cm × 10 cm loaf tin and cover again with greased plastic wrap. Set aside until the dough reaches the top of the tin. Brush with milk to glaze.
6. Bake at 200°C for 35–40 minutes or until the loaf sounds hollow when tapped from underneath.
7. Transfer the bread to a cake rack. Brush the topping butter over the top of the loaf and sift the icing sugar on top while the butter is still moist (to give a thick layer of icing sugar that does not float away). Allow to cool.

By hand
Sponge the yeast as described in step 1. Sift the flour, salt and sugar into a large bowl. Stir through the lemon rind and raisins. Rub in the butter and make a well in the centre. Pour in the frothy mixture and mix. Once almost all the flour has been absorbed, turn the dough out onto a lightly floured board and knead well for 10 minutes until the dough is smooth. Continue from step 4.

Variations:
• Use mixed peel and orange rind.
• Use currants or sultanas in place of raisins.

This recipe is an adaption of one I tasted at American chef Joanne Weir's cooking class held in Auckland.

1¼ tsp dried yeast or 4 tsp Surebake	1 tblsp sugar
1¼ cups warm water	70-gram pkt walnut pieces
2 tblsp good quality olive oil	¼ cup good quality olive oil
pinch sugar	½ tsp minced garlic
3 cups high grade flour	4-6 sprigs fresh rosemary, chopped
1 tsp salt	100 grams grapes (green or black)

Walnut and fresh grape focaccia

2 rounds

1. Sprinkle the yeast over the water and stir in the first measure of olive oil and the pinch of sugar. Leave in a warm place for 15 minutes or until the mixture is frothy.
2. Put the flour, salt and sugar into a food processor and pulse to sift.
3. With the motor running, pour the frothy liquid down the feed tube and continue processing the soft dough for 1 minute. Add more liquid if necessary.
4. Turn the dough out onto a floured board and bring together. Turn the dough over in a large greased bowl and cover with greased plastic wrap. Leave in a warm place for 1 hour or until double in bulk.
5. While the dough is rising, chop the walnuts. They should not be fine, but should not be large pieces either. Heat the second measure of olive oil in a frying pan and add the walnuts, garlic and rosemary. Cook for 3-4 minutes over a moderate heat or until the walnuts are golden and toasted and the oil has a heady aromatic rosemary flavour.
6. Knock the dough down and turn out onto a floured board. Place half the grapes on top of the dough and fold over and roll — to squash the grapes into the dough.
7. Divide the dough in half and roll each half out to a 20-23 cm round and place on a greased baking tray. Set aside for 20 minutes.
8. Sprinkle the walnut oil mixture evenly over the doughs and squash the remaining grapes evenly into the dough. Press the tips of your fingers into the dough to make the traditional focaccia dents as well.
9. Bake at 220°C for 20 minutes or until golden brown and crisp. Serve warm. Great with smoked meats, like venison, beef or chicken; serve with a salad of crisp bitter lettuce leaves.

By hand
Sponge the yeast as outlined in step 1. Sift the flour, salt and sugar into a large bowl and make a well in the centre. Gradually mix in the frothy liquid and when all the flour is almost absorbed, turn the dough out onto a lightly floured board and knead well for 10 minutes until the dough is smooth. Continue from step 4.

Variation:
Use half wholemeal and half plain flour.

Cook's Tips:

Nuts should always be kept in the freezer as they have a high oil content and will go rancid if left in a warm place.
Rosemary is a strong herb, use it cautiously.

Chocolate coffee cake

With tiny morsels of chocolate in a rich sweet dough and a caramelised base, this cake is ideal to enjoy over coffee with family and friends.

1 tblsp dried yeast or 3 tblsp Surebake
1 cup warm milk
3 cups high grade flour
1 tsp salt

25 grams butter
¼ cup caster sugar
2 eggs
½ cup chocolate chips

Topping
75 grams butter
¼ cup demerara or raw sugar
1 tsp ground ginger

1. Sprinkle the yeast over the warm milk and leave it in a warm place for 15 minutes until the mixture is quite frothy.
2. Put the flour, salt and butter in a food processor and process 1 minute. Add the sugar and pulse to mix.
3. Beat the eggs and add to the frothy yeast mixture. With the motor running, gradually pour the yeast mixture down the feed tube and process to form a soft dough. Process for 1 minute. Add more liquid if necessary.
4. Pulse in the chocolate chips. Turn the dough out onto a floured board and bring together.
5. Turn the dough over in a large greased bowl and cover with greased plastic wrap. Set aside in a warm place for about 1 hour or until the mixture has doubled in bulk.
6. Turn the dough out and knock back. Shape the dough into 16 even balls.
7. Beat topping ingredients together and spread over the base of a 23 cm cake tin. It must not be a loose-bottomed tin.
8. Place the balls of dough into the tin in an even formation. Cover with plastic wrap and leave until they have doubled in bulk, about 40-50 minutes.
9. Bake at 200°C for 30 minutes or until cooked.
10. Turn out onto a large platter to serve with coffee.

By hand
Sponge the yeast as described in step 1. Sift the flour and salt into a large bowl. Rub in the butter and stir through the sugar and chocolate chips. Make a well in the centre. Add the eggs to the yeast mixture and gradually mix into the flour. Once almost all the flour has been absorbed, turn the dough out onto a lightly floured board and knead well for 10 minutes until the dough is smooth. Continue from step 5.

Variations:
- Use fruit instead of chocolate chips.
- Use another spice in the topping.
- Use brown sugar in place of demerara or raw sugar.

Opposite: Blue Cheese Loaf (page 146), Basil and Tomato Loaf (page 148).

This is a one-rise recipe. Rising bread twice will ensure a better texture, but often we need a quick to make loaf. Try this one — it is a softer dough than the standard loaf.

Linseed bread

1¼ tsp dried yeast or 4 tsp Surebake
1 cup warm water
1 tsp sugar
1 cup high grade flour
1½ cups wholemeal flour
1 tsp salt

2 tblsp milk powder (optional)
50 grams butter
½ cup linseeds
2 tblsp treacle
extra warm water

Topping ideas
¼ cup linseeds, oat flakes, oat bran, pumpkin seeds or sunflower seeds or a mixture of
    these

1. Stir the yeast into the warm water and sugar and set aside for 15 minutes until frothy.
2. Put the flour, wholemeal flour, salt and milk powder (if using) into a food processor and pulse to sift.
3. Add the butter and process until rubbed in. Pulse in the linseeds.
4. Add the treacle to the frothy yeast mixture.
5. With the motor running, pour the liquid down the feed tube as fast as the flour can absorb it and process to a very soft dough. Add any extra water if required. The mixture should be tacky.
6. Process for 1 minute.
7. Transfer the dough to a well greased and floured 20 cm × 10 cm loaf tin. Sprinkle over one of the topping ingredients.
8. Cover with greased plastic wrap and wrap in a towel. Leave in a warm place for 1 hour or until the loaf is double in bulk.
9. Bake at 200°C for 30-35 minutes or until the loaf sounds hollow when tapped underneath. Cool on a cake rack.

Cook's Tip:

Add milk powder to help enrich the flavour of the dough. If you do not have it, feel free to omit it.

By hand
Sponge the yeast as described in step 1. Add the treacle. Sift the flour, salt and milk powder into a bowl. Rub in the butter and stir through the linseeds. Make a well in the centre and gradually pour in the frothy yeast mixture. Once most of the flour has been absorbed, turn the dough out onto a lightly floured board and knead well for 10 minutes until the dough is smooth. Continue from step 7.

Variation:
In place of linseeds use pumpkin seeds, sunflower seeds or a combination of the two.

Opposite (from top to bottom): Coconut and Honey Pancakes (page 139), Golden Wholemeal Pancakes (page 140), Chocolate Pancakes (page 138), Basic Pancakes (page 140).

Honey-scented white bread

This is my standard bread recipe that I have made for years, with honey and milk powder added to enrich its flavour. Variations on this are really up to you. My favourites are at the end of the recipe.

1½ tsp dried yeast or 1½ tblsp Surebake
1 cup warm water
1 tsp sugar
2 tblsp honey (I use creamed)
3 cups high grade flour

2 tblsp soft butter
2 tblsp milk powder
1 tsp salt
extra water
milk to glaze

1. Sprinkle the yeast over the warm water and stir in the sugar. Leave in a warm place for 15 minutes or until very frothy. Stir in the honey.
2. In a food processor put the flour, butter, milk powder and salt, and pulse to sift.
3. With the motor running, gradually pour the frothy liquid down the feed tube until it is all incorporated and a soft dough is formed. Add more water if needed.
4. Turn the dough out onto a floured board and bring together. Place in a greased bowl, turn over and cover with greased plastic wrap. Set aside for 1 hour or until double in bulk.
5. Turn the dough out and knock back. Shape the dough into a loaf and place in a greased 20 cm × 10 cm loaf tin.
6. Cover with greased plastic wrap and leave in a warm place for about 30–45 minutes until the dough is level with the top of the tin, or has doubled in bulk. Brush with milk and dust lightly with flour.
7. Bake at 220°C for 30 minutes or until the loaf sounds hollow when tapped from underneath. Turn out onto a cake rack to cool.

By hand
Sponge the yeast as described in step 1. Sift the flour, milk powder and salt into a large bowl. Rub in the butter and make a well in the centre. Gradually mix in the frothy yeast mixture and once the flour has been almost absorbed turn out onto a floured board and knead well for 10–15 minutes until the dough is smooth. Continue from step 4.

Cook's Tip:

Turn dough over in a greased bowl when proving to give the whole dough a light covering of oil or butter so that parts of the dough will not stick and be torn away when you remove it from the bowl.

Variations:
• Use half wholemeal and half plain flour.
• Add ½ cup linseeds, poppy seeds, sunflower seeds or raisins.
• Add chopped and fried bacon, parsley and ½ cup finely diced cheese.
• Omit the honey if wished and add treacle.
• Add chopped herbs.
• Dust the top with oat bran, rolled oats or oat flakes.

Presentation variations:
• Divide the dough in half and place both halves in the tin. This was my favourite bread as a child and there would be a fight with my brother

Adrian about who would get the soft part in the middle when the loaves were quickly torn apart.

- Make the dough into rolls. Bake at the same temperature for about 15 minutes.
- Glaze the bread if wished with milk for a deeper colour if not covering with flour.
- Bake the dough on a greased tray in the shape of a round (called a cob loaf).
- Divide the dough into three even pieces. Roll them out to long sausages and plait. Bake in the tin or on a tray.

Cook's Tip:

To tell if a loaf is cooked, take it out of the tin (with gloves on hands) and tap it underneath. If it sounds hollow, it is cooked. If not, return to the oven.

Cook's Tips:

- *To get a deep shine on bread, brush with a little beaten egg mixed with salt and allow to stand for 2 minutes and then brush again before baking.*

- *If the tops of bread or cakes begin to brown too quickly within the first 10 minutes of cooking, cut open a paper bag (if you can find one — they're mostly plastic these days!) and place it on top. Use parchment if you do not have brown paper.*

- *To make a decorative finish with poppy or sesame seeds, dip your thumb in water or milk and then into the seeds. Press them into the top of a bread loaf in a decorative fashion.*

- *Potato flour dusted on top of a loaf before baking will craze and crack haphazardly into unique patterns when baking.*

- *Adding skim milk powder to dough adds colour to the crust and acts as a tenderizer. You will need no more than ¼ cup to a standard two-loaf recipe. If the recipe does not call for it, remove the same measure in flour and replace with the milk powder.*

- *Do not allow a skin to form when proving, as this will keep the dough from rising. Turn the dough over in a greased bowl, cover with greased plastic wrap and put aside in a warm place to rise. If the dishwasher is going, I place it on the bench over the machine; the heat from that is about right.*

Hot cross buns

16 buns

The origin of hot cross buns is misty. The story I like the most talks about buns that were given to travellers with a cross cut into the top to ward off evil they might encounter on their journey. This story goes back to pagan times. Another Anglo Saxon story tells us that fruit buns were eaten at spring festivals in honour of the fertility goddess, Eostere, and the cross was added in early Christian times to represent the cross of Christ. Whichever story is true, hot cross buns are wonderful when enjoyed with family and friends at Easter.

4 cups high grade flour
1 tsp salt
½ tsp each ground allspice, mixed
  spice, cinnamon and nutmeg
¼ cup brown sugar
1½ tsp dried yeast or 1½ tblsp Surebake

1 cup warm milk
2 eggs
100 grams softened butter
1 cup mixed dried fruit

Crosses
½ cup flour
¼ tsp baking powder
1 tblsp butter
milk

Glaze
2 tblsp sugar
2 tblsp milk

1. Put the flour, salt, spices and brown sugar into a food processor and pulse to sift.
2. Stir the yeast and milk together and set aside in a warm place for 15 minutes or until the mixture is frothy.
3. Beat the eggs and softened butter into the frothy mixture.
4. With the motor running, pour the yeast mixture down the feed tube as fast as the flour can absorb it to form a soft dough. Process the mixture for 1 minute. Add the dried fruit and pulse to blend.
5. Turn the dough over in a greased bowl and cover with greased plastic wrap. Set aside in a warm place for about 1 hour until the dough has doubled in bulk.
6. Turn out onto a lightly floured board and divide into 16 equal portions. Roll into balls and place on a greased baking tray with about 1 cm between each bun.
7. Cover with a clean teatowel and set aside in a warm place for about 30 minutes until well risen. Brush with milk.
8. Pipe thin crosses onto the buns.
9. Bake at 190°C for about 20-25 minutes.
10. Brush with the sugar glaze just before they come out of the oven. Cool on a cake rack.

Crosses
Mix the flour and baking powder together and rub in the butter. Stir in sufficient milk to make a thick batter that can be piped.

Glaze
Dissolve the sugar in the milk.

By hand
Sponge the yeast as outlined in steps 2 and 3. Sift the flour, salt, spices and brown sugar into a large bowl and stir through the dried fruit. Make a well in the centre. Gradually mix in the frothy yeast mixture. Once most of the flour has been absorbed, turn the dough out onto a lightly floured board and knead well for 10 minutes until the dough is smooth. Continue from step 5.

Cook's Tips:

Crosses were traditionally cut into the buns, not piped. Cut the crosses after you have brushed the buns with milk before baking.
If using trim milk when sponging yeast, always add ¼ tsp sugar to give the yeast food to grow on.

Cook's Tip:

To work out the amount of Surebake to use in place of dried yeast, basically triple the dried yeast quantity called for. It may not always be 100 per cent, but I find it the easiest rule of thumb on this issue.

Bagels

16 bagels

Bagels get their unique chewy texture from being poached in water before being baked. Bagels are the cornerstone of the popular Jewish snack of bagels, lox (smoked salmon) and cream cheese. They are even more delicious with fresh dill and black pepper.

1 tblsp dry yeast or 3 tblsp Surebake
2 cups warm water
1 tsp sugar
4 cups high grade flour
2 tsp salt

extra water
3 tblsp sugar
1 egg
¼ cup poppy or sesame seeds

1. Sprinkle the yeast over the water and stir in the sugar. Set aside for 15 minutes or until the mixture becomes very frothy.
2. Put the flour and salt into a food processor and pulse to mix.
3. With the motor running, pour the liquid down the feed tube gradually until all the liquid is incorporated and a moist dough is formed. Add more liquid if necessary. Process 1 minute.
4. Turn the dough out onto a floured board and bring together. Place in a large greased bowl. Cover with greased plastic wrap and leave in a warm place for one hour or until the dough has doubled in bulk.
5. Turn the dough out onto a floured board and knock back. Shape the dough into 16 even pieces and roll each into a ball.
6. Push your finger through the centre of each ball of dough and twirl the dough around your finger to make a large hole. (It should be almost large enough to get your fist through.) Place the rounds on a floured board or cloth and cover with a dusting of flour and a clean teatowel. Leave to rise for 25 minutes. The bagels will be well risen and the centre hole now about the size of your second finger.
7. Bring a large saucepan of water to the boil and stir in the 3 tablespoons sugar. Put 1 bagel into the saucepan at a time and cook for 30 seconds on each side. Remove with a slotted spoon and place on a greased baking tray.
8. Beat the egg with a pinch of salt and brush the bagels with the egg glaze. Sprinkle with the poppy seeds.
9. Bake at 200°C for 15-20 minutes or until the bagels sound hollow when tapped underneath. Cool on a cake rack.

By hand

Sponge the yeast as described in step 1. Sift the flour and salt into a large bowl and make a well in the centre. Gradually mix in the liquid and once most of the flour has been absorbed turn the dough out onto a lightly floured board and knead well for 10-15 minutes until the dough is smooth. Continue from step 4.

Variations:
- Top bagels with sesame seeds or pumpkin seeds or a mixture of whole grains.

- Add ¼ cup finely diced and sautéed onion to the dough for a soft onion-flavoured bagel.

What went wrong

- **No Flavour**
Bread needs salt. Don't forget to add it. Salt also helps control the action of the yeast. If left out, the dough can rise too fast and have an uneven texture. Do not be concerned about the salt/health issue in these recipes. One teaspoon per recipe is of little consequence when a loaf feeds 4-5 people.

- **Dough Does Not Rise**
This can be one of several reasons; these are the main ones.

  Yeast: It is dead. All the recipes in my book state to dissolve the yeast first and allow it to sponge. If it does not froth up (sponge), throw it out. It is dead. This procedure is the same for dry yeast or compressed.

  Dough too soft: If the dough is too soft and sticky, it will not have enough flour in it to give it body and to hold a shape when you mould it. If your dough is too sticky, you can knead more flour into the dough little by little.

  Dough too firm: Too much flour will not allow the dough any elasticity and the dough will have difficulty in rising. If your dough is tough and refuses to be kneaded, gradually add water (about 1 tablespoon at a time) and knead it in until the dough becomes pliable. It will take time, but you can correct the problem.

  Insufficient kneading: When a recipe calls for dough to be kneaded for 10-15 minutes until it is elastic and smooth, it really means that length of time. This is why I prefer the food processor, which requires only a good minute to a minute-and-a-half to ensure the dough is well kneaded.
  The kneading of the dough develops the gluten (flour protein), making it malleable and helping it to form thousands of little cells that entrap the gas and expand. If you are kneading dough by hand, stretch the dough out, roll up, turn and slam down on the bench and repeat.

This process was taught to me when I was training, and it helps activate the gluten and aerates the dough at the same time.

When the dough has been proving, if you push your finger into the dough and the indent remains, then the dough has been allowed sufficient time to prove.

- **Top of the Bread is Burnt**

  If your dough is too dark on top and soft and pale at the bottom, the loaf has been too close to the top of the oven. Choose an oven position that will allow room for the loaf to rise without burning. A middle to upper-middle oven position is fine for tall loaves.

- **Crust Has Burst or Separated**

  I have to admit that I quite like this in a loaf of homemade bread, so I never worry about it too much. However it is caused by not allowing the bread sufficient resting time at both stages: the gases have been unable to escape and the loaf top has separated to allow this to happen (to avoid this, slash the top of the loaf). Or, a skin was allowed to form on the loaf during the second rising and this has separated from the loaf. Another explanation is that the oven was too low.

- **Holey Bread**

  The dough was overmixed. This is particularly important when making doughs in a food processor, and practice will make perfect here. Or, the dough was allowed to become too warm — again, you need to be careful when using a food processor as the temperature of the machine can over-heat the dough.

  If after all of this your dough still fails, then it was the kitchen devils at work! Practice will ensure enjoyment and success in bread baking. Look for more tips throughout the chapter.

PANCAKES

A lazy Sunday brunch isn't complete without pancakes, is it! Pancakes also make the quickest dessert, or a winter filler for families. I make no excuses for not liking the thin crepe variety from France. No, I prefer thick but ever-so-light American pancakes, topped with bacon and maple syrup — decadent but delicious, especially in winter!

Pancakes were probably the first kind of bread that we ate and can be found the world over. In Russia they are made with buckwheat and called blini; in France they are thin and called crepes; in Hungary they are palacsinta. In the States people refer to them as flapjacks, while to Britons and descendants they are called pancakes.

A fun tradition not often followed today is the eating of pancakes on Shrove Tuesday, which was the day when the faithful were 'shriven' or granted absolution after confession in preparation for the solemnities of Lent. The pantry was emptied of all food ready for the austere time ahead and pancakes were consumed with much fun and frivolity on the Tuesday before Lent began. Thank goodness we can have them all year round. Enjoy this selection of my favourite combinations.

Buttery sour cream pancakes

6 pancakes

The sour cream in this recipe provides the necessary fat content to achieve a light pancake. The browned butter gives the most wonderful nutty taste.

1½ cups self rising flour
¼ cup caster sugar
pinch salt
50 grams butter

250-gram tub sour cream
1 cup water
2 egg whites

1. Sift the flour, sugar and salt into a bowl and make a well in the centre.
2. Heat the butter in a small pan and cook it until it begins to brown. Remove from the heat and stir in the sour cream and water.
3. Pour the liquid into the well and using a whisk incorporate into the flour, beating until smooth.
4. In a clean bowl, whisk the egg whites until soft peaks form and fold into the batter.
5. Pour ¾ cupfuls of the mixture into a hot greased pan and cook until the bubbles on the surface begin to burst. Then flip the pancake and cook the other side for about 1–2 minutes. Serve hot with your favourite topping.

Pancakes freeze well. Place a piece of paper between each layer — this will help separate them when they are defrosting.

Cook's Tips:

Butter cooked until it is light brown and added to batter imparts a unique, wonderful flavour. It is standard in pancake recipes in my home.
If you do not have sour cream, sour the same amount of cream with 1 teaspoon lemon juice or cider vinegar and allow to stand for 10 minutes.
Self rising flour makes a lighter pancake. If you do not have it, use pure flour and 1 teaspoon baking powder to each cup.

Chocolate pancakes

6 pancakes

Serve these for dessert with strawberries and ice cream. They are delicious.

1½ cups self rising flour
¼ cup cocoa
pinch salt
¼ cup caster sugar

2 eggs
1 cup water
¾ cup milk
pinch cream of tartar

1. Sift the flour, cocoa, salt and sugar into a bowl and make a well in the centre.
2. Separate the eggs and beat the yolks together with the water and milk.
3. Gradually pour the liquid into the well and stir with a whisk until the mixture is smooth.

4. In a clean bowl beat the egg whites with the cream of tartar until soft peaks form. Fold into the batter.

5. Pour ¾ cupfuls of the batter into a greased pan. When the tiny bubbles on the surface begin to burst, turn the pancakes over and cook the other side for about 1-2 minutes. Stack on top of one another and serve them warm. They probably will be eaten as they are cooked.

Cook's Tip:

The flavour of cocoa or chocolate will be enhanced if the recipe uses water, as fat masks the chocolate flavour.

Coconut and honey pancakes

6 pancakes

Made with fresh coconut cream, these pancakes have a lovely subtle coconut flavour which goes well with peaches, apricots, bananas and mangoes.

I used the Paradise brand which is fresh chilled coconut cream but you can also use tinned varieties

1¾ cups self rising flour
pinch salt
3 eggs

300 ml coconut cream
3 tblsp liquid honey
pinch cream of tartar

1. Sift the flour and salt into a bowl and make a well in the centre.

2. Separate the eggs and beat the egg yolks, coconut cream and honey together. Using a whisk, gradually stir the liquid into the flour to form a smooth batter.

3. In a clean bowl whisk the egg whites with cream of tartar until they form soft peaks. Gradually fold into the batter.

4. Cook ¾ cupfuls of the mixture in a hot greased pan. When the bubbles on the surface begin to burst, flip the pancake over and cook the other side for about 1-2 minutes. Serve hot.

Cook's Tip:

To incorporate the liquid in pancakes without making too many lumps, pour the liquid in gradually and stir with the whisk as you go. Do not over beat as it will make a tough batter. I find a whisk easier than a wooden spoon, but use a wooden spoon if you do not have a whisk.

Golden wholemeal pancakes

6 pancakes

Wholemeal flour adds a nutty taste to these pancakes. They are gently sweetened with a little golden syrup, which adds a distinctive flavour.

1 cup self rising wholemeal flour
½ cup plain self rising flour
pinch salt
3 eggs

2-3 tblsp golden syrup
1 cup milk
pinch cream of tartar

1. Mix the flours and salt together in a large bowl and make a well in the centre.
2. Separate the eggs and beat the egg yolks together with the golden syrup and milk. Using a whisk, stir the liquid into the flour to make a smooth batter.
3. In a clean bowl whisk the egg whites with the cream of tartar until they form soft peaks. Fold the egg whites into the batter.
4. Cook ¾ cupfuls of the mixture in a hot greased pan. When the bubbles on the surface begin to burst, turn the pancake over and cook the other side for about 1-2 minutes. Serve hot with lemon juice and caster sugar.

Cook's Tip:

Do not use all wholemeal flour as it will make a heavy pancake.

Basic pancake

6 pancakes

I make my basic pancakes (also my favourite recipe) with buttermilk, which is now readily available in supermarkets and is great for baking. It makes a lovely light pancake, with a great tangy taste that I prefer.

1½ cups self rising flour
pinch salt
50 grams butter

3 eggs
2 cups buttermilk
pinch cream of tartar

1. Sift the flour and salt into a bowl and make a well in the centre.
2. Melt the butter and cook until it is nut brown in colour.
3. Separate the eggs and mix the egg yolks with the buttermilk.
4. Pour the buttermilk mixture into the well and mix gradually with a whisk until incorporated. Whisk in the melted butter.
5. In a clean bowl whisk the egg whites with cream of tartar until they form thick soft peaks. Fold into the batter.
6. Cook ¾ cupfuls of the batter in a hot greased pan. When the bubbles on the top of the surface begin to burst, turn the pancake over and cook the other side for a further 1-2 minutes.

Cook's Tip:

If you do not have buttermilk, use milk. It will make a good pancake but have a slightly different texture and taste.

Variations:

- Add blueberries or other chopped fresh fruit. It is best to add the fruit to the pancakes just after you have poured the mixture into the pan, sprinkling about 3-4 tblsp over the top. Otherwise you will find they sink to the bottom of the batter in the bowl and add more liquid to the batter than required.
- Add grated lemon rind to the batter (the rind of about two lemons will give a full lemony flavour).

Toppings for pancakes

These are some of my favourites (they are pretty well known I'm sure, but that's because they taste great).

- Bacon, not too crispy, with maple syrup or golden syrup
- Lemon juice with sugar (everyone's favourite)
- Honey with fresh fruit
- Raspberry or apricot jam and whipped cream

Basic crepes

6-8 crepes

These thin crepes are best for making into pancake stacks, be they sweet — filled with poached fruits, covered with caramel topping and grilled before being cut into wedges — or savoury — filled with a meat or vegetarian filling and topped with cheese and herbs. They are also the traditional pancake for Crepes Suzette, which is a lovely dessert.

½ cup flour
pinch salt
1 egg
about ¾ cup milk

1. Sift the flour and salt into a bowl and make a well in the centre.
2. Beat the egg and milk together and strain to remove any lumps of egg.
3. Using a whisk, gradually pour the liquid into the well, stirring to make a smooth batter. The batter should be of pouring consistency. Add extra milk if necessary.
4. Strain the batter into a jug and allow to stand for about 30 minutes.
5. Pour sufficient batter into the base of a hot greased pancake pan so that when the batter is rotated to cover the base it covers it only with a thin layer.
6. When the pancake surface begins to look dull on the top and the bottom is brown, flip the pancake over and cook the other side only until it is browned, about 30 seconds. Stack the pancakes on top of each other until ready to use.

Cook's Tip:

Pancakes freeze well. Place a piece of paper between each layer — this will help separate them when defrosting.

LOAVES

Loaves are usually easier to make than cakes. In this chapter there is a collection of the healthy and not-so-healthy — my favourite is the Banana and Papaya Bread.

A good flavoured loaf, sliced thickly and topped with butter, is a popular treat that doesn't take long to make. Easy-to-cut loaves are particularly good for school lunch boxes too.

Fruit loaves that last long enough to become stale are wonderful toasted and topped with butter and your favourite jam.

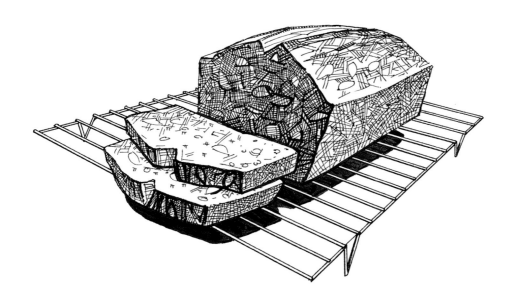

This recipe comes from my girlfriend Louise, who also shared her chocolate cake recipe with us. Louise has a penchant for strong smoky teas, and often serves this flavoursome loaf to friends at 'chat times'. I am sure you will enjoy it too.

Louise's ginger loaf

2 cups pure flour	½ cup caster sugar
1½ tsp baking soda	½ cup boiling water
1½ tsp ground ginger	½ cup golden syrup
1 tsp cinnamon	½ cup melted butter
½ tsp salt	1 egg, beaten

Glaze
½ cup icing sugar
juice 1 lemon

1. Sift the flour, baking soda, ginger, cinnamon, salt and sugar into a large bowl and make a well in the centre.
2. Mix together the boiling water, golden syrup and melted butter and pour into the well. Add the beaten egg and mix with a holed spoon to make a smooth batter.
3. Transfer mixture to a greased, floured and lined 21 cm × 9 cm loaf tin.
4. Bake at 180°C for 35 minutes or until a skewer inserted comes out clean.
5. Allow to stand in the tin for 10 minutes before turning out onto a cake rack to cool. Spread the top with the glaze. Cut into slices to serve. Store in an airtight container.

Glaze
Mix together the icing sugar and lemon juice.

Cook's Tip:

Do not over beat mixtures like this as you will cause the loaf to peak. To mix, gradually lift the mixture and fold.

Honey nut marmalade bread

2½ cups self rising flour	2 eggs
½ tsp salt	1 tblsp grated orange rind
2 tblsp butter	2 tblsp orange juice
½ cup honey	1 cup chopped walnuts or pecans
1 cup orange marmalade	

1. Sift the flour and salt into a large bowl.
2. Rub in the butter until the mixture looks like fine crumbs.
3. In a separate bowl beat together the honey, marmalade, eggs, orange rind, juice and walnuts or pecans.
4. Stir the liquid ingredients into the sifted dry ingredients.
5. Turn the mixture into a greased, floured and lined 21 cm × 9 cm loaf tin.
6. Bake at 180°C for 40-50 minutes or until a cake skewer inserted comes out clean.
7. Allow to cool in the tin for 10 minutes before turning out to cool on a cake rack. If wished, serve the loaf dusted with icing sugar or drizzle over a little orange icing. Store in an airtight container.

Cook's Tip:

Make a quick orange icing with the juice of an orange and icing sugar mixed to a smooth consistency.

Orange poppy seed bread

This loaf is particularly good toasted and buttered.

2 cups self rising flour	1 egg
½ tsp salt	¾ cup milk
2 tblsp poppy seeds	1 tblsp freshly grated orange rind
2 tblsp melted butter	¼ cup chopped apricots
½ cup orange marmalade	2 tblsp sieved orange marmalade

1. Use a fork to combine flour, salt and poppy seeds in a large bowl. Make a well in the centre.
2. Beat together melted butter, marmalade, egg, milk, orange rind and chopped apricots.
3. Pour the liquid ingredients into the well. Stir the batter with a holed spoon until it is just combined.
4. Transfer the batter into a well greased, floured and lined 21 cm × 9 cm loaf tin.
5. Bake at 180°C for 45-50 minutes, or until a skewer inserted comes out clean.
6. Brush top of loaf with sieved marmalade. Let loaf cool for 10 minutes before turning out onto a cake rack to cool. Serve sliced with butter. Store in an airtight container.

Onion bread

This recipe is adapted from a recipe in one of my favourite books, *Middle Eastern Cookery* by Arto der Haroutunian (Pan Books). Labelled 'the bread of the poor', it has a flavour everyone will enjoy.

1 onion	½ tsp chilli powder
3 cups self rising flour	1 tsp chopped fresh thyme
1 tsp salt	3-4 tblsp tapenade
2 tsp baking powder	½ cup oil (light oil such as peanut)
1 tsp cumin	1½ cups milk

1. Peel and finely dice the onion.
2. Sift the flour, salt, baking powder, cumin and chilli powder into a bowl.
3. Stir in the fresh thyme, tapenade and onion.
4. Make a well in the centre and add the oil and milk and mix with a knife to make a sticky dough.
5. Turn the dough into a greased, floured and lined 21 cm × 9 cm loaf tin.
6. Bake at 180°C for 30-35 minutes or until well risen and golden. Cool on a cake rack. Serve warm with savoury foods. Store in an airtight container when cold.

Variations:
- Add chopped rosemary and anchovies to the dough.
- Make the bread with equal quantities of wholemeal flour and plain flour.

Opposite: Lemon Syrup Loaf (*left*) (page 145), Date Loaf (page 148).

- Make a topping of sautéed onion, a little garlic and fresh herbs, such as thyme and rosemary, and sprinkle on top before baking.

Loaves are not usually iced, but a lemon icing often make a loaf more special

Cook's Tip:

Tapenade is a wonderful olive paste prepared from olives, anchovies and olive oil. If you do not have any, use chopped olives.

Lemon syrup loaf

Made tastier by the tangy lemon syrup that is poured over it after cooking, this loaf is absolutely delightful.

¾ cup caster sugar
2 eggs
125 grams butter
1¾ cups self rising flour

pinch salt
½ cup milk
½ cup chopped walnuts (optional)
2 tblsp grated lemon rind

Syrup
¼ cup lemon juice
2 tblsp sugar
drop vanilla essence

1. Put the sugar and eggs into a food processor and process.
2. Add the butter and process until thick.
3. Pulse in the flour, salt, milk, walnuts and lemon rind.
4. Transfer the mixture to a greased, floured and lined 21 cm × 9 cm loaf tin.
5. Bake at 180°C for 40-50 minutes or until a cake skewer inserted comes out clean.
6. Leave in the tin and pour syrup over while hot. Allow the loaf to stand in the tin for a further 10 minutes before transferring to a cake rack to cool. Slice and serve, buttered if wished. Store in an airtight container.

Syrup
Dissolve the lemon juice and sugar together with the vanilla essence, and pour over the loaf.

Hand/electric beater method
Cream butter, sugar and lemon rind until light and creamy. Add eggs one at a time and beat well. Sift the flour and salt and fold into the creamed mixture with the milk and walnuts.

Opposite: Bread and Butter Pudding with Whisky Sauce (page 171).

Blue cheese loaf

With a mild blue cheese flavour and scented with fresh herbs, this is a great savoury loaf. Serve sliced, toasted and topped with salad and salami.

2 cups self rising flour
½ tsp baking powder
½ tsp salt
¾ cup plain unsweetened yoghurt
¼ cup milk
1 egg

75 grams melted butter
¼ cup grated cheddar cheese
50 grams blue cheese
2 tblsp finely chopped herbs
2 tblsp chopped walnuts (optional)
¼ cup extra grated cheese

1. Sift together the flour, baking powder and salt.
2. In a separate bowl blend together the yoghurt, milk, egg, melted butter, cheddar cheese, crumbled blue cheese and chopped herbs.
3. Carefully stir the liquid ingredients into the dry ingredients.
4. Turn the mixture into a well greased, floured and lined 21 cm × 9 cm loaf tin. Sprinkle the walnuts and extra grated cheddar cheese on top.
5. Bake at 180°C for about 35-40 minutes or until a cake skewer inserted comes out clean. Store in an airtight container.

Variations:
- Omit the blue cheese and add an extra ¼ cup grated cheddar cheese.
- Use half wholemeal self rising flour and half plain self rising flour.

Apple and ginger tea bread

This recipe appeared in *Next*, and we served it with slices of gouda or edam cheese. This makes an ideal snack for hungry school children.

1 egg
1 cup brown sugar
1 tblsp golden syrup
125 grams butter
1 tsp baking soda
¼ cup milk

1 cup pure flour
½ cup wholemeal flour
½ cup ground oats or oat bran
1 tsp baking powder
1½ tsp mixed spice
2 cooking apples

1. Put the egg, sugar and golden syrup into a food processor and process for 1 minute until light and creamy. Add the butter and process until well mixed.
2. Dissolve the baking soda in the milk.
3. Sift the flour. Sprinkle sifted flour, wholemeal flour, oats, baking powder and mixed spice over the top of the creamed mixture with the milk.
4. Peel, core and dice the apples. Sprinkle on top. Pulse to mix all ingredients.
5. Turn the mixture into a well greased, floured and lined 12 cm × 23 cm loaf tin.
6. Bake at 180°C for 60-70 minutes or until a skewer inserted comes out clean.

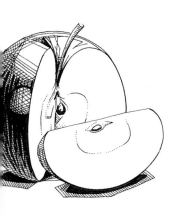

7. Leave the loaf in the tin for 10 minutes before turning out onto a cake rack to cool. Cut into slices and serve with cheese. Store in an airtight container.

Hand/electric beater method

Beat the butter, brown sugar and golden syrup together until creamy. Add the egg and beat well. Sift the dry ingredients together and fold into the creamed mixture with the apples and milk.

Variation:

Use pears instead of apples and spice the loaf with ginger or cardamom.

Bran and fruit loaf

These loaves have become very popular, with various types of bran cereals as one of the main ingredients. I have seen this recipe in many places and this is my version of it. I very rarely use wholemeal flour as I feel there is enough fibre in the loaf with the San-Bran.

2 cups San-Bran
1 cup sugar
2 cups milk
1 tblsp golden syrup or treacle
2 cups flour

2 tsp baking soda
1 tsp mixed spice
½ tsp ground ginger
1 cup mixed dried fruit

1. Put the San-Bran, sugar, milk and golden syrup or treacle into a bowl and leave to soak for 2 hours or overnight.
2. Sift together the flour, baking soda, mixed spice and ground ginger.
3. Mix the dried ingredients into the soaked San-Bran and stir in the dried fruit.
4. Pour the mixture into a greased, floured and lined 21 cm × 9 cm loaf tin.
5. Bake at 180°C for 40 minutes or until a skewer inserted comes out clean.
6. Cool in the tin for 10 minutes before turning out onto a cake rack to cool. Store in an airtight container.

Variation:

Change the fruit and spices for different flavours.

Cook's Tip:

Fruit loaves will freeze well. Ensure they are well wrapped and then place in a freezer bag and seal tightly. Allow to defrost at room temperature.

Date loaf

Yes, but it isn't boring!! I remember as a child how often this loaf would find its way onto the table; I began to wonder if any other kind of loaf recipe existed. But it has grown on me over the years and I enjoy a slice when it is a few days old and well flavoured.

1 cup chopped dates	¾ cup caster sugar
1 tsp baking soda	1 egg
1 cup boiling water	2 cups self rising flour
2 tblsp butter	½ cup chopped walnuts (optional)

Choose moist sweet dates for best results. Dried hard dates while soaked never seem to have as much flavour

1. In a bowl mix together the dates, baking soda and hot water and allow the mixture to stand for 1 hour or until cool.
2. Beat the butter and sugar together. (The mixture will not cream but it needs to be well mixed.)
3. Lightly beat the egg and gradually add to the butter mixture.
4. Sift the flour. Stir the date mixture into the creamed mixture and lastly stir in the flour and nuts (if using).
5. Turn into a well greased, floured and lined 21 cm × 9 cm loaf tin.
6. Bake at 180°C for about 40 minutes or until a skewer inserted comes out clean.
6. Allow to stand in the tin for 10 minutes before turning out onto a cake rack to cool. Store in an airtight container.

Variations:
- Use raisins in place of dates.
- Add 2 tablespoons finely chopped crystallized ginger.

Basil and tomato loaf

This is a real American-style loaf with sweet and savoury flavours all mixed together. It is best on the day it is baked, still warm and buttered with unsalted butter. Try it topped with slices of smoked beef.

3 medium-sized tomatoes	3 eggs
1 spring onion	125 grams softened butter
1 tblsp tomato paste	1 cup self rising wholemeal flour
6 basil leaves	1 cup self rising flour
1 tsp grated fresh ginger	1 tsp baking soda
1 cup caster sugar	pinch salt

1. Quarter and de-seed the tomatoes. Discard the seeds. Trim the spring onion.
2. In a food processor put the tomatoes, spring onion, tomato paste, basil leaves, ginger and sugar and process until the mixture is smooth.
3. Add the eggs and softened butter and process the mixture for 1 minute.
4. Sift together the flours, baking soda and salt and sprinkle evenly over the

top of the ingredients in the processor. Pulse to mix.

5. Turn the mixture into a well greased, floured and lined 21 cm × 9 cm loaf tin.

6. Bake at 180°C for 50-60 minutes or until a skewer inserted comes out clean.

7. Allow to cool in the tin for 10 minutes before turning out onto a cake rack to cool. Store in an airtight container.

Earl Grey tea loaf

The flavour of this loaf can easily be changed depending on the type of tea you use. I enjoy Earl Grey but my girlfriend Louise, whose Ginger Loaf is in this chapter, prefers Lapsang Souchong, a very pungent tea from the Fujian province of China.

¾ cup mixed dried fruit
¼ cup finely chopped dried apricots
½ cup sugar
1 cup hot strong Earl Grey tea

1½ cup self rising flour
½ cup self rising wholemeal flour
½ tsp grated nutmeg
1 egg

1. Toss the dried fruit, apricots and sugar together. Pour the hot tea over the fruit and leave for 1 hour or until cool.

2. Sift the flours and nutmeg together.

3. Beat the egg into the cooled fruit mixture. Carefully stir in the flour.

4. Transfer the mixture to a well greased, floured and lined 21 cm × 9 cm loaf tin.

5. Bake at 180°C for 30 minutes or until a skewer inserted comes out clean.

6. Allow to cool in the tin for 10 minutes before turning out onto a cake rack to cool. Store in an airtight container.

Variations:

- Add 1 teaspoon mixed spice to the recipe (or any spice combination that you like).
- Use dried prunes in place of apricots.
- Add a teaspoon of caraway seeds.

Cook's Tip:

Loaves are cooked at moderate temperatures, as heavy dense batters in large amounts take time to heat through to cook. If you try to speed the time up by cooking a loaf at a higher temperature, it will not be well risen and may be crusty and cracked on the top.

Banana and papaya bread

3/4 cup caster sugar
3 eggs
150 grams butter
2 bananas
1/4 tsp vanilla essence
2 tsp baking powder

2 tblsp milk
1 1/4 cups wholemeal self rising flour
1 cup plain self rising flour
pinch salt
1/2 cup dried papaya

1. Put the sugar and eggs into a food processor and process for 1 minute until the mixture is light and creamy.
2. Add the butter and process until the mixture is creamy.
3. Mash the bananas and pulse into the creamed mixture with the vanilla essence.
4. Stir the baking powder into the milk and pulse into the banana mixture.
5. Pulse in the flours, salt and papaya.
6. Turn into a greased, floured and lined 21 cm × 9 cm loaf tin.
7. Bake at 180°C for about 45-50 minutes or until a skewer inserted comes out clean.
8. Allow the cake to cool in the tin for 10 minutes before turning out onto a cake rack to cool. Store in an airtight container.

Variations:
- Omit the papaya and add walnuts or pecans.
- Add a little spice such as ginger. Even cinnamon would add a new flavour.

Hand/electric beater method
Cream the butter and sugar together. Add the eggs and beat well. Mash the bananas. Mix the baking powder and milk together. Fold the sifted dry ingredients into the creamed mixture with the bananas, milk, vanilla and papaya.

Cook's Tip:
Bananas are found in all sizes. For this recipe I use 2 medium-sized bananas that are well ripened. If you are using large bananas, either eat half of one or add a few more minutes to the cooking time!

CHOCOLATE

Chocolate cakes come three ways: delicious, rich and wicked (all equate to pure ecstasy!).

Never feel guilty about eating a chocolate cake, never! I am sure that chocolate was put on earth purely for self-indulgence and enjoyment. I had never been a great fan of it until I began to put these recipes together. They are a collection of the best flavoured chocolate cakes you could hope to enjoy, some rich, some delicious, but mostly wicked. I am now a converted chocoholic!

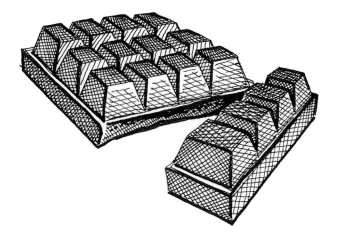

Mississippi mud cake

This is so fabulously rich, a dusting of icing sugar is all that is needed.

2 tsp instant coffee
1¼ cups hot water
¼ cup whisky or fruit juice
175 grams cooking chocolate
250 grams unsalted butter
2 cups sugar

2 cups pure flour
1 tsp baking soda
2 eggs
1 tsp vanilla essence
icing sugar to dust with

1. Put the coffee, hot water, whisky or fruit juice into a saucepan and bring to a simmer.
2. Add the broken chocolate and butter and stir until melted. Add the sugar and stir until the sugar has dissolved.
3. Remove the mixture from the heat and allow to cool.
4. Sift the flour and baking soda together into a large bowl and make a well in the centre.
5. Beat the eggs together with the vanilla and stir into the chocolate mixture.
6. Pour the chocolate mixture into the well in the dry ingredients and stir to mix.
7. Pour the mixture into a well greased and floured 23 cm ring tin.
8. Bake at 140°C for 1½-1¾ hours until the cake has shrunk from the sides of the tin and is firm to the touch.
9. Cool in the tin for 20 minutes before turning out onto a cake rack to cool.
10. Dust with icing sugar before serving.

Louise's chocolate cake

This simply scrumptious chocolate cake recipe has great flavour. It hails from a close friend, Louise, who is a wonderful cook, especially of fast good-tasting Italian foods, in particular tapenade and foccacia! This is her stand-by chocolate cake, usually devoured after the main course. Louise maintains that it is best made with an electric beater, though making it in the food processor will give acceptable results. Processor instructions are at the end of the recipe.

175 grams unsalted butter
1½ cups caster sugar
2 eggs
2 tblsp golden syrup

1½ tsp baking soda
1½ cups self rising flour
1½ tblsp cocoa
1½ cups milk

1. Beat the butter and sugar together until the mixture is very light and creamy and the butter has become very pale.
2. Add the eggs one at a time and beat well after each addition. Beat in the golden syrup.

3. Sift together the baking soda, flour and cocoa and fold into the creamed mixture alternately with the milk.

4. Turn the mixture into a well greased, floured and lined 23 cm round cake tin.

5. Bake at 180°C for 50-60 minutes or until a skewer inserted comes out clean.

6. Cool in the tin for 10 minutes before turning out onto a cake rack to cool.

7. When cold, ice with chocolate butter icing or decorate with whipped cream.

Food processor method

Put the eggs and sugar into the food processor and process until light and creamy. Add the butter and golden syrup and process for 2 minutes. Sift the flour, cocoa and baking soda and sprinkle evenly on top of the creamed mixture. Pour in the milk and pulse to mix. Do not over mix.

Mayonnaise chocolate cake

Yes, it's an American recipe. Who else would use mayonnaise? But it works well. Mayonnaise is a mix of egg yolk and oil, which are common ingredients in baking. Choose a good quality mayonnaise that is not overly flavoured for best results!

¼ cup cocoa	1 cup caster sugar
1 cup hot water	2 cups pure flour
1 tsp vanilla essence	2 tsp baking soda
¾ cup mayonnaise	

1. Put the cocoa, hot water and vanilla essence into a small bowl and mix together. Allow to cool.

2. In a food processor, put the mayonnaise, caster sugar, flour, baking soda and the cooled cocoa mixture. Process for 1 minute.

3. Pour the mixture into a well greased, floured and lined 20 cm cake tin.

4. Bake at 180°C for 25-30 minutes or until the cake is cooked. Do not be alarmed if the cake drops slightly in the middle — it's okay.

5. Cool in the tin for 10 minutes before turning out onto a cake rack to cool.

6. Ice with chocolate butter icing if wished or serve with whipped cream. Store in an airtight container.

Variations:
• Add ¼ cup finely chopped nuts or dates.
• Add 1 tblsp coffee powder for a mocha version.

Chocolate layer cake

Very rich and absolutely delicious, this is a recipe I picked up while working in Seattle.

150 grams cooking chocolate
1 cup milk
1 cup caster sugar
1 tsp vanilla essence
125 grams unsalted butter

3 eggs, separated
2 cups pure flour
1 tsp baking soda
pinch salt

Icing

100 grams cooking chocolate
397-gram tin condensed milk
125 grams unsalted butter

1 egg yolk
vanilla essence to taste

1. In the top of a double boiler put the chocolate and milk and heat until the chocolate has melted.
2. Remove from the heat and stir in the sugar and vanilla essence. Allow the mixture to cool completely.
3. Beat the butter until light and creamy. Gradually beat in the chocolate mixture and egg yolks until all combined.
4. Sift the flour, baking soda and salt together and stir into the chocolate mixture.
5. Beat the egg whites together until stiff but not dry. Add the caster sugar and beat until the sugar has dissolved.
6. Fold the meringue mixture into the chocolate mixture, being careful not to over mix.
7. Divide the mixture evenly between two well greased, floured and lined 23 cm round cake tins.
8. Bake at 180°C for 25–30 minutes or until a cake skewer inserted comes out clean.
9. Allow the cakes to cool in the tin for 20 minutes before turning out on a cake rack to cool.
10. Split each cake in half and fill with icing, leaving enough icing to decorate the top.

Icing

Melt the chocolate in the top of a double saucepan or in the microwave. If using a saucepan then remove from the heat. Stir in the condensed milk and butter, adding a small amount at a time. The butter is not to melt while being added. Beat in the egg yolk and vanilla essence to taste. Continue beating until warm then leave to cool completely before using to ice the cake.

Coffee and chocolate marry so well. This cake has a wicked frosting — beware!

Rich mocha cake

1 cup caster sugar
¼ cup brandy or water
2 tblsp instant coffee powder
175 grams cooking chocolate
2 tsp vanilla essence

150-gram pkt walnuts
1 slice white toast bread
125 grams unsalted butter
6 eggs, separated
½ tsp cream of tartar

Butter frosting

175 grams cooking chocolate
¼ cup water
1 tblsp instant coffee

3 egg yolks
250 grams unsalted butter
¾ cup icing sugar

1. Put the sugar, brandy or water, coffee, chocolate and vanilla into the top of a double saucepan and cook over simmering water until the chocolate has melted and the sugar has dissolved. Allow to cool.
2. Process the walnuts and the bread in a food processor until the walnuts have turned to very fine crumbs.
3. Put the butter and egg yolks into the food processor and process until the mixture is creamy.
4. Process in the cold chocolate mixture.
5. In a clean bowl whisk the egg whites with the cream of tartar until they form stiff but not dry peaks.
6. Fold the chocolate mixture into the egg whites with the walnuts and bread.
7. Turn into a well greased, floured and lined 28 cm round cake tin, or two 20 cm cake tins.
8. Bake at 180°C for 25–30 minutes until the cake is firm to the touch.
9. Cool in the tin for 10 minutes before turning out onto a cake rack to cool.
10. To serve, cut the cake in half horizontally. Spread half the butter frosting on one piece of cake and cover with the other piece of cake. Cover the top with remaining butter frosting and decorate with chocolate coated coffee beans. Serve at room temperature.

Butter frosting
Put the chocolate, water and coffee into the top of a double saucepan and heat gently until the chocolate has melted. Allow to cool thoroughly. Add the egg yolks and beat well. Beat the butter and icing sugar until creamy, then beat in the cold chocolate mixture. (Wicked!)

Cook's Tip:

Store chocolate tightly wrapped in a cool dry place. Warm temperatures will cause a 'bloom', or a mottled or streaked surface to occur. This is the cocoa butter rising to the top. It will not affect the chocolate.

Cracked chocolate cake

This is a quick and interesting cake. It will crack like nothing else on top when it's cooked — but don't worry, it's supposed to. Dust with plenty of icing sugar to serve.

100 grams chocolate (dark, milk or white)
100 grams butter
5 tblsp flour
¾ cup caster sugar
3 eggs
about ¼ cup icing sugar

1. Melt the chocolate and butter in a double saucepan or in the microwave. It will take about 1 minute on high power.
2. Beat together the flour, caster sugar and eggs with an electric beater until thick and creamy.
3. Gradually beat in the melted chocolate and butter mixture.
4. Pour into a well greased and lined 23 cm loose-bottom cake tin. Bake at 180°C for 60 minutes until the mixture is set.
5. Allow to cool in the tin before removing to a plate.
6. Serve with vanilla cream (see Chocolate Decadence recipe).

Chocolate hazelnut torte

I was originally going to cover this cake with a rich white chocolate icing and decorate it with chocolate-coated hazelnuts. But it was so light that a heavy butter cream was not right. Give the torte a liberal dusting of icing sugar and serve it with whipped cream flavoured with Frangelico and Kahlua.

1 cup whole hazelnuts
1 cup pure flour
125 grams cooking chocolate
175 grams unsalted butter
4 eggs
1 cup caster sugar

Cook's Tip:

The skin on hazelnuts is quite bitter, so always remove it before cooking.

1. Toast the hazelnuts in a 180°C oven for about 15 minutes or until the hazelnuts begin to smell toasted. Allow to cool thoroughly until they are cold enough to handle and you can rub their skins off.
2. Process the hazelnuts in a food processor until they are finely ground. Add the flour and pulse to mix well.
3. Melt the chocolate and butter together in the top of a double saucepan just until the chocolate has melted. Allow to cool.
4. In a clean bowl beat the eggs and sugar together until the mixture is pale and thick. This will take about 10 minutes if you use a hand beater.
5. Beat in the chocolate and butter mixture.
6. Fold in the flour and hazelnuts.
7. Pour the mixture into a greased, floured and lined 20 cm cake tin.
8. Bake at 180°C for 40-45 minutes until the cake is firm to the touch. Move the cake; if the centre still wobbles, the mixture is not cooked. The top may become meringue-like and crack, but this is okay.

9. Cool in the tin for about 1 hour before turning out onto a cake rack to cool thoroughly.

Chocolate fudge cake

Not so decadent, but a richer family cake made in minutes! It has to be good.

1 cup cocoa
1¼ cups hot water
3 eggs
250 grams unsalted butter

2 tsp vanilla essence
3 cups self rising flour
1¼ tsp baking soda
2 cups brown sugar

Icing
2 tblsp cocoa
1 tblsp butter, melted
1 cup icing sugar
hot water

1. Mix the cocoa and hot water together and beat until smooth. Allow to cool thoroughly.
2. In a food processor put the cooled cocoa mixture, eggs, butter, vanilla essence, flour, baking soda and sugar. Process together for 3 minutes.
3. Pour the mixture into a well greased and floured 25 cm ring tin.
4. Bake at 180°C for about 1 hour or until the cake is cooked when tested with a skewer.
5. Allow to cool in the tin for 10 minutes before turning out onto a cake rack to cool.
6. Ice with quick chocolate icing, or serve as an afternoon-tea cake with whipped cream flavoured with brandy or Drambuie.

Quick chocolate icing
Mix the cocoa with melted butter, icing sugar and sufficient hot water to make a thick spreadable icing.

Cook's Tip:
While chocolate can be melted with other liquid, if it is melted alone and even a single drop of moisture then falls in, the chocolate will 'seize' or harden. You can solve this by immediately stirring in 1 tblsp of oil to every 175 grams chocolate, then slowly re-melting it.

Buttermilk chocolate layer cake

Buttermilk gives a contrasting sharpness to this chocolate layer cake.

125 grams dark cooking chocolate
2 cups pure flour
1½ tsp baking soda
1 tsp baking powder
1 cup caster sugar

250 grams unsalted butter
4 eggs
1 tsp vanilla essence
1 cup buttermilk

Chocolate butter icing

3 tblsp hot water
¼ cup cocoa
1 tsp vanilla essence
100 grams unsalted butter

2 cups icing sugar
300-ml bottle cream
extra icing sugar
8 walnut halves or 8 strawberries

1. Break up the chocolate and melt in the top of a double saucepan or in the microwave.
2. Sift together the flour, baking soda and baking powder.
3. Put the sugar, butter, eggs and vanilla essence into a food processor and process until the mixture is light and creamy. Add the cold chocolate mixture and process to mix.
4. Sprinkle the flour mixture on top of the creamed mixture with the buttermilk and pulse to mix. Do not over process.
5. Pour the mixture evenly into 2 well greased, floured and lined 23 cm cake tins.
6. Bake at 180°C for 35–45 minutes until the cake is cooked.
7. Cool in the tin for 10 minutes before turning out onto a cake rack to cool.
8. Split each cake in half horizontally. Layer with ¼ of the chocolate butter icing and ⅓ of the whipped cream, finishing with a layer of chocolate butter icing. Decorate with walnuts or strawberries.

Chocolate butter icing

Mix the hot water, cocoa and vanilla essence together and set aside until very cool. Beat together the cocoa mixture, butter and sifted icing sugar. Whip cream until thick and sweeten if wished.

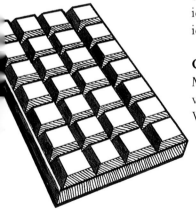

Cook's Tip:

Unsalted butter is a must to allow the flavour of chocolate to be its best.

Sour cream chocolate fudge cake

125 grams butter
100 grams cooking chocolate
2 cups brown sugar
3 eggs
½ tsp vanilla essence

2½ cups pure flour
2 tsp baking soda
1 cup light sour cream
¾ cup boiling water
2 tblsp icing sugar

1. Put the butter and chocolate in large bowl. Melt by placing over hot water or in the microwave.
2. Add brown sugar, eggs and vanilla essence. Beat with a wooden spoon until smooth and thick.
3. Sift the flour and baking soda. Add the sifted mixture and sour cream to the eggs. Stir with a wooden spoon until combined.
4. Add boiling water and stir until mixed in.
5. Pour into a greased 22 cm ring tin. Bake at 160°C for 50-60 minutes or until cooked and firm to touch.
6. Cool and remove from tin.
7. Serve dusted with icing sugar. Alternatively, drizzle chocolate icing over the cake.

Cook's Tip:

Be careful when melting chocolate in a microwave. It can burn easily, so check it regularly.

Peanut and chocolate chip cake

This one will certainly be a favourite with children. The combination of peanuts and chocolate is an all-time winner.

125 grams butter
1 cup caster sugar
3 eggs
1¼ cups whole blanched peanuts

½ cup chocolate chips
1½ cups self rising flour
¼ cup milk

1. Melt the butter. Add the caster sugar and eggs. Beat with a wooden spoon until smooth.
2. Roughly chop peanuts (either in a food processor or by hand).
3. Add peanuts, chocolate chips, flour and milk to butter mixture. Stir until ingredients are mixed together.
4. Spread into a greased 20 cm square tin.
5. Bake at 180°C for 40 minutes or until the cake feels cooked when lightly touched and has begun to shrink from the sides of the tin.
6. Cake may be left plain or iced with chocolate icing.

Cook's Tips:

Peanuts may be more finely chopped if you prefer smaller pieces in the cake.
Use walnuts in place of peanuts for a variation.

Chocolate decadence with vanilla cream

I was introduced to this recipe in Seattle, USA, when I was working there researching an exciting food programme. It is truly decadent and will feed a large number of people. I would suggest accompanying it with poached fruits or fresh berries to counter-balance the richness.

500 grams unsalted butter
500 grams cooking chocolate
6 eggs lightly beaten
½ cup sugar

1 cup sifted cocoa powder
2 cups almonds, ground and toasted
  lightly
¼ cup Amaretto liqueur

Vanilla cream

1 cup cold milk
1 piece vanilla bean or 1 teaspoon
  vanilla extract

3 extra large eggs
¼ cup sugar
½ cup heavy cream

Cook's Tip:

A bain marie is a water bath. You will need a dish larger than the one you are cooking the Decadence in. Place this in the oven. Add the Decadence and then gradually fill the larger dish with cold water until the water comes about ½ way up the sides of the cake tin. Always add cold water, as it heats gently allowing an even dispersion of heat to the pudding.

1. Slice the butter and transfer it to the top of a double boiler. Chop the chocolate coarsely, add it to the double boiler and melt them together. When melted, remove from the heat and allow to cool.
2. Beat the eggs with the sugar until light and then beat in the cooled chocolate mixture.
3. Stir in the cocoa powder and almonds. Add the Amaretto.
4. Pour the batter into a well greased and lined 23 cm × 23 cm cake tin. Smooth the surface evenly.
5. Bake in a bain marie for 40 minutes or until a knife comes out clean when inserted in the centre.
6. Cool on a rack for 2-3 hours before transferring to a refrigerator for 4-6 hours.
7. Serve with vanilla cream.

Vanilla cream

Simmer the milk with the vanilla bean for five minutes. Cool. In a glass bowl, stir the eggs and sugar with a wooden spoon until the sugar is incorporated and the yolks become a pale yellow. Stir in the warm milk. Transfer the mixture to the top of a saucepan of simmering water (a double boiler) and cook over a moderate heat, stirring until the cream has thickened. Continue to stir away from the heat for 2-3 minutes until cool. Transfer the sauce to a wine bottle or other narrow container. Cork the bottle and refrigerate for 1 hour or longer. This sauce may be prepared up to two days in advance. Makes 2 cups.

Variations:

*   Use half ground hazelnuts and half toasted almonds, and replace Amaretto with Frangelico.
*   For the vanilla cream, add the grated rind of a lemon when cooked to add a citrus flavour.

Opposite: Burnt Mango and Apple Strudel (page 181).

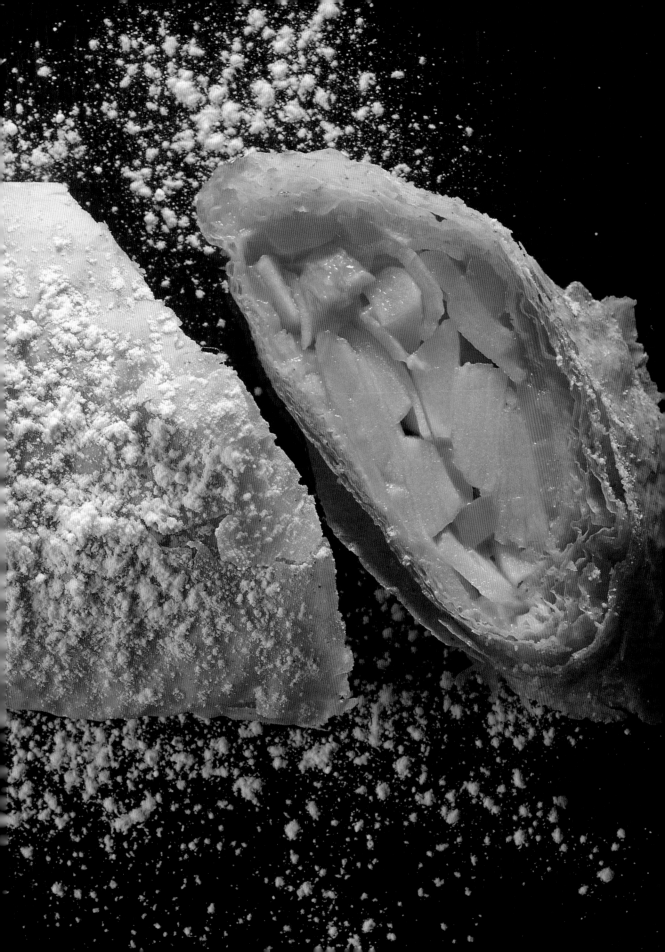

Anything made with white chocolate is totally and utterly irresistible to me. It's not that I hunt out white chocolate recipes, they just seem to be in the way more than I would like. Oh, for some simple willpower occasionally. This is delicious, rich and wickedly wonderful!

White chocolate and lemon cake

250 grams white chocolate
1 cup cream
3 eggs
175 grams unsalted butter
1 cup caster sugar

1 cup flour
½ cup cornflour
1 tsp baking soda
1 tsp baking powder
grated rind of 1 lemon

White chocolate and lemon frosting

75 grams white chocolate
50 grams butter
grated rind of 1 lemon

2 cups icing sugar
½ cup cream cheese

1. Put the white chocolate and cream together in the top of a double saucepan and cook over a moderate heat until the chocolate has melted. Remove from the heat and allow to cool well.
2. Put the eggs, butter and caster sugar into a food processor and process for about 3 minutes until the mixture is creamy.
3. Add the cooled chocolate mixture and pulse to blend.
4. Sift over the flour, cornflour, baking soda, baking powder and lemon rind and pulse to mix.
5. Turn the mixture into two well greased, floured and lined 23 cm cake tins.
6. Bake at 180°C for about 40 minutes until the cakes are cooked and golden.
7. Allow to cool in the tin for 15 minutes before turning out onto a cake rack to cool.
8. Ice with white chocolate and lemon frosting.

White chocolate and lemon frosting

Chop the white chocolate roughly and melt over hot water. Cool well. Beat together the butter, white chocolate, lemon rind, icing sugar and cream cheese.

Cook's Tip:

You can use quark instead of cream cheese in the frosting, but when you've done this much damage to calorie control, there really seems little point!

Opposite: Creamy Plum Tart (page 174).

White chocolate and chestnut pavé

Serves 20

This is beyond understanding until you try it. It really deserves to be in the wicked category. Pavé is French for paving stone, and no name could be more appropriate to describe this ultra-decadent recipe. I designed this recipe when I was teaching at the Epicurean Cookschool in Auckland for a Decadent Desserts class, which was quickly booked out!

400 grams white chocolate	¼ cup brandy
75 grams unsalted butter	3 eggs
½ cup caster sugar	1 egg yolk
430-gram can unsweetened chestnut purée	½ cup cream
2 tblsp cornflour	

Coating
50 grams unsalted butter
25 grams each white chocolate and dark chocolate

1. Put the chocolate, butter and sugar into the top of a double saucepan and stir over a moderate heat until all the ingredients have melted. This can be done in a microwave but be careful as white chocolate will burn quickly. Allow the chocolate mixture to cool for about 10 minutes.
2. Process the chestnut purée in a food processor until smooth.
3. Add the cooled chocolate mixture and process until just blended. Do not over process.
4. Add the cornflour, brandy, eggs, egg yolk and cream and pulse to mix.
5. Pour the mixture into a lightly oiled Balmoral cake tin or a 22 cm × 10 cm loaf tin.
6. Bake at 180°C for 40 minutes until firm.
7. Allow the pavé to cool for about 1 hour before putting in the refrigerator for at least 8 hours to set firmly.
8. Loosen from the cake tin by quickly dunking the tin into hot water. Do not hold it too long. Turn out onto a serving platter.
9. Melt half the coating butter with each portion of the chocolate so that you have two colours. Coat the pavé in alternate strips of white and dark chocolate, or however you would like to. If the pavé is cold, the chocolate will set quickly.
10. Serve in small portions (it is so rich it will serve about 20) with poached or fresh fruits.

Everyone has an outrageous friend, someone who throws caution to the wind, tries everything and anything, and succeeds or fails with great laughter and much fun. My girlfriend Debbie is one of these people. Her company, and food, brightens any day. Deb's cake has a truly wicked rating, and is a fabulous finish to a meal.

Debbie's chocolate fudge cake

500 grams dark cooking chocolate
250 grams unsalted butter
1 tsp vanilla essence
6 eggs (separated)
6 tblsp caster sugar

1. Chop the chocolate and butter roughly and place into the top of a double saucepan over gently simmering water. When melted, stir in the vanilla essence and remove from the heat.
2. Quickly stir the egg yolks into the chocolate.
3. Beat the egg whites in a clean bowl until stiff but not dry. Beat in the sugar, 1 tablespoon at a time, until you have a thick meringue mixture.
4. Take 2-3 large spoonfuls of the meringue mixture and stir into the chocolate mixture. Then gradually fold the chocolate mixture into the egg whites.
5. Turn into a greased and lined 23 cm loose-bottom cake tin. Bake at 180°C for 45 minutes.
6. Remove from the oven and allow to stand for 15 minutes.
7. Invert the cake onto a serving platter, leaving the base of the tin on top of the cake but removing the outside ring. Place a weight on top. I used 2–3 dinner plates, as they apply even pressure and are an easy weight to find. Leave for at least 2 hours. Then remove the plates, tin base and paper. Cover with sifted icing sugar and serve in very small wedges. Do not refrigerate, but keep in a cool place.

Cook's Tip:

If you get a piece of egg shell in the egg whites when separating eggs, the easiest way to get it out is with another piece of egg shell. Hold it near and the fragment will be drawn into the shell. Trying to get it out with a utensil will take forever.

DESSERTS

When I was a kid, dinner was never served without a dessert or pudding. Usually milk-based, it was cooked at the same time as the other components of the meal to be cost and time efficient. In those days my mum never wasted a thing — something I'm pleased she taught me. Left-over boiled rice was served in a Baked Queen Pudding; windfall fruits were stewed and turned into crumbles and pies. It was these warm and wonderful puds that gave me my love of desserts.

Today, more often than not, a piece of fruit, a bowl of yoghurt or some cheese and crackers take the place of desserts. When I entertain, however, I go all out to make something wonderfully enjoyable for everyone.

It's sad that desserts and puddings have become part of the entertaining menu and are not included more in family meals. Desserts do not have to be fancy nor do they have to be 'fattening', an issue I have very strong feelings about. They can be simple, quick to prepare and good for the family. Enjoy puddings or desserts in moderation and in context with other parts of your meal and diet.

This chapter has a mix of ideas, some for family and some for entertaining. Many are old favourites with twists to make them exciting dinner-party fare. On a wintry night I enjoy the look on my guest's faces when I serve up Oxtail Casserole and a Bread and Butter Pudding! All those wonderful memories of childhood seem to become instant topics of conversation.

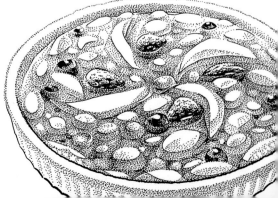

Baked jam roll

Serves 6

Do you remember this one? It's great winter comfort food, served with lashings of custard or whippped cream, especially before an open fire on a Sunday night. There are any number of variations and I have listed a few at the end.

125 grams softened butter   milk
2 cups self rising flour   about ½ cup apricot jam

Syrup
½ cup sugar   ½ cup boiling water
50 grams melted butter

1. Rub the butter into the flour until the mixture resembles fine crumbs.
2. Add sufficient milk to make a soft dough.
3. Turn out onto a lightly floured board and bring together.
4. Roll out to about 1 cm thickness and spread with the apricot jam, leaving a 1 cm edge all the way around. Roll up like a swiss roll and place in a greased oven-proof dish (such as a casserole dish).
5. Make the syrup by stirring together the sugar, butter and boiling water. Pour over the roll.
6. Bake at 180°C for 45 minutes until the roll is golden and well risen.
7. Serve sliced with a little of the sauce and custard or cream.

Variations:
*   Add chopped dried or fresh apricots to the jam.
*   Use one grated apple in place of the jam.
*   Make the syrup with half water and half lemon juice.
*   Make the roll with half wholemeal and half plain flour.
*   Add grated lemon or orange rind to the syrup.

I occasionally make this with 1 ½ times the sauce recipe but beware you need a bigger dish

Baking blind technique

Many recipes call for being 'baked blind', or baked without a filling. We do this when the filling requires little or no cooking time, or is added later. It also helps to cook the pastry without it becoming soggy.

1. Prick the base of the pastry lining with a fork to let air escape.
2. Cover the base with a circle of greaseproof or baking paper, and put in a temporary filling of dried beans, rice or metal beans to prevent the pastry rising. (My dried beans have been used for years.)
3. Bake in the centre of a preheated oven at the temperature stated in the recipe.
4. When the pastry has cooked for the stated time, remove the lining and the temporary filling. Set the temporary filling aside to cool. Return the flan to the oven for 2-3 minutes to dry pastry out.
5. Store the temporary filling material in a covered jar for later use when cold. Do not put away when warm as they will steam and become mouldy.

NOTE: Metal beans can be purchased from specialist kitchen shops for the purpose of baking blind, but are expensive when compared to dried kidney or haricot beans!

Blackberry and chocolate self-saucing pudding

Serves 8

Adding a punnet of blackberries to this self-saucing chocolate pudding gives a new dimension.

1½ cups self rising flour
2 tblsp cocoa
100 grams butter
½ cup sugar

1 cup milk
1 tsp vanilla
1 punnet blackberries

Sauce
2 tblsp cocoa
½ cup sugar
2 cups boiling water

1. Sift the flour and cocoa into a bowl. Rub in the butter until the mixture resembles fine crumbs. Stir in the sugar.
2. Make a well in the centre and add the milk and vanilla essence and mix with a holed spoon to form a stiff mixture.
3. Fold in the blackberries. Turn the mixture into a greased 6-cup capacity oven-proof dish.
4. Mix the sauce ingredients together and pour over the batter.
5. Bake at 180°C for 45 minutes or until cooked.
6. Serve hot with lashings of whipped cream.

Variations:
• Use carob in place of cocoa.
• Omit the cocoa in the batter and have a marbled pudding.
• Omit the blackberries for a standard self-saucing chocolate pud.

Feijoa ginger sponge pudding

Serves 4-6

Fruit sponges are very simple to make and add interest to stewed fruits. Vary the base with whatever fruit is in season — I have listed some combinations below.

8-10 feijoas
1 cup water
2 tblsp sugar
4 whole cloves
1 cup flour
1½ tsp ground ginger

1½ tsp baking powder
100 grams butter
½ cup caster sugar
1 egg
½ cup milk

1. Peel the feijoas and trim the ends.
2. Cut into thick slices and place in a saucepan with the water, sugar and cloves.
3. Simmer for 5-7 minutes until soft.
4. Using a slotted spoon, transfer the fruit to an oven-proof dish.
5. Boil the remaining poaching liquid down until only 2-3 tablespoons remain. Strain this over the fruit.

6. Sift the flour, ginger and baking powder together.
7. Beat the butter and sugar until light and creamy.
8. Lightly beat the egg into the creamed mixture.
9. Sift and fold the dry ingredients alternately with the milk into the creamed mixture.
10. Spoon over the fruit. Level the top.
11. Bake at 180°C for 30-35 minutes or until the sponge is well cooked and golden.

Variations:
- Apple and passionfruit.
- Pear with ginger.
- Raspberry and apple.
- Rhubarb and orange.
- Berry compote.

Peach surprise

Serves 6

If you keep a packet of cake mix on hand in your cupboard for real emergencies, then this recipe may come in handy one day. I enjoy it made with fresh fruits as well as tinned. Use plums or firm berry fruits, such as blackberries or keriberries.

1 packet plain cake mix *1 tsp orange rind*
½ cup coconut *2 tblsp orange juice*
100 grams melted butter *1 egg*

Filling
425-gram can sliced peaches, drained

Topping
250-gram tub sour cream *2 tblsp orange juice*
1 egg *cinnamon*
1 tsp ginger

1. Combine cake mix, coconut, melted butter, orange rind and juice, and egg together to form a dough. Press into a well greased and floured 23 cm flan dish.
2. Bake at 180°C for 30 minutes.
3. Arrange sliced peaches over cooked base.
4. For the topping, combine sour cream, egg, ginger and orange juice and pour on top of peaches.
5. Bake at 180°C for a further 20 minutes until the topping has set and is lightly coloured.
6. Serve dusted with cinnamon.

Pecan pie

Serves 8

Pecans are about as American as the Stars and Stripes and Apple Pie. This popular tart is rich and delicious, warm in winter with custard or cold in summer with cream or yoghurt.

1¼ cups pure flour
1 tblsp icing sugar
100 grams butter
about 3 tblsp cold water

Filling

75 grams butter
¼ cup golden syrup
½ cup brown sugar
2 eggs

½ cup pure flour
½ tsp baking powder
2 × 70-gram pkt dessert pecans

1. Place the flour and icing sugar in a food processor.
2. Add the butter and process until the mixture resembles fine crumbs.
3. Pulse in sufficient water until the mixture forms smooth moist balls of dough. Turn out and bring together.
4. Roll pastry out to fit the base and sides of a 23 cm flan dish. Refrigerate 20 minutes. Bake blind for 10–12 minutes while preparing the filling★.
5. Melt the butter. Add the golden syrup, brown sugar and remove from the heat. Add the eggs and stir quickly to mix together well.
6. Add the flour, baking powder and one packet of the pecans (which have been chopped).
7. Pour the filling into the prepared base. Arrange the rest of the pecans in a circular pattern on top.
8. Bake at 200°C for 10 minutes and then lower the heat to 180°C for a further 15 minutes, or until the tart is golden and firm to the touch.

*See the introduction for the baking blind technique.

Lemon tart

Serves 8

A refreshing citrus tart with plenty of bite. I enjoy anything lemon in a dessert. This recipe could also be made into small individual tarts.

1½ cups flour
pinch salt
150 grams butter
about ¼ cup cold water

Filling

3 eggs
¾ cup caster sugar
1 cup cream

½ cup lemon juice
½ cup orange juice
grated rind of 1 lemon

1. Put the flour and salt into a food processor and pulse to sift.
2. Add the butter and process until the mixture resembles fine crumbs.

3. Pulse in sufficient water until the mixture forms small moist balls of dough.
4. Turn out and use to line the base and sides of a 23 cm flan dish. Refrigerate for 20 minutes. Bake blind while preparing the filling★.
5. Lightly beat the eggs with a fork. Add the caster sugar, cream, lemon and orange juice, and lemon rind and beat well to combine.
6. Pour the filling into the centre of the prepared flan and smooth out.
7. Bake at 180°C for about 45 minutes or until the filling is just set.

*See the introduction for the baking blind technique.

Outrageous pecan toffee pud

Serves 8

I'm known for my love of over-the-top desserts and this is one of them. Ridiculously rich but scrumptious, this is just the best thing for those cold winter evenings.

1½ cups chopped dates
1 cup boiling water
2 tsp coffee
1 tsp vanilla essence
¾ tsp baking soda

175 grams butter
1 cup caster sugar
3 eggs
1½ cups self rising flour

Sauce
¾ cup brown sugar
125 grams butter
¼ cup cream
70-gram pkt pecans

1. Put the dates, water, coffee, vanilla essence and baking soda into a large bowl. Allow to stand for 10 minutes.
2. Beat the softened butter and sugar together until light and fluffy. The sugar should have dissolved.
3. Add the eggs one at a time, beating well with each addition.
4. Sift the flour and carefully mix into the creamed mixture with the dates. The batter should be alarmingly sloppy — don't panic, it's okay.
5. Pour the mixture into a well greased 23 cm ring tin.
6. Bake at 180°C for 30 minutes, until a skewer inserted comes out clean. Leave to stand while preparing the sauce.
7. Turn the pudding out onto a large heat-proof dish and pour the sauce over the top. Place under a hot grill for 2–3 minutes until the sauce has caramelised. Serve with extra cream. (By this point there is no use me telling you to have it with yoghurt, but that would be nice.)

Sauce
Put the sugar, butter, cream and chopped pecans into a saucepan and simmer together for 5 minutes.

Cook's Tip:

Make the pud and sauce in advance. To reheat, allow the pud 1 minute in the microwave on full power and then pour over the sauce and place under the grill.

Brown sugar meringue

Serves 6

Traditionally, meringues are made with caster sugar. Using brown sugar adds new flavour to this family favourite.

4 eggs
½ cup brown sugar

Filling

¼ cup lemon juice
1 tsp finely grated lemon rind
½ cup sugar
50 grams butter

300 ml cream
2–3 oranges
100 grams black grapes

1. Draw 2 × 20 cm circles on a large sheet of greaseproof paper, and brush circles with melted butter.
2. Separate the eggs. Whisk the egg whites until stiff, but not dry. Sift the brown sugar, a little at a time (discarding any lumps) into the egg whites, whisking after each addition, until the sugar is absorbed.
3. Pipe or spoon the meringue mixture over the circles. Bake at 120°C for 2 hours, when the meringue will be dry.
4. In a microwave-proof bowl combine lemon juice, lemon rind, sugar and butter (cut into small cubes) and microwave on high for 1½ minutes. Beat the egg yolks and whisk into the hot lemon mixture, then microwave on high for 1 minute or until slightly thickened. Allow to cool.
5. Whisk the cream until it stands in soft peaks, then carefully fold into the cool lemon honey.
6. Sandwich the meringues together with the filling. Spread a thin layer over the top of the meringue.
7. Decorate with orange segments and black grapes. With a large star nozzle, pipe swirls of lemon cream around the edge of the gateau. If you do not have a piping bag, spoon the cream into small mounds around the top of the gateau.

Cook's Tip:

Assemble the gateau about 3 hours before serving, so that the meringue has softened.

Cook's Tip:

Any traces of grease or egg yolk will stop egg whites from beating up. It's best to wash the bowl in hot water and dry with a clean teatowel. A pinch of cream of tartar will help too.

Absolute decadence! A great family favourite, and with the whisky sauce, it becomes something special. A white cob loaf with a hard crust (from the bread shop) is the best bread to use, as it will give the pudding a better texture. If this isn't available, use thick sliced bread.

2-3 tblsp softened butter
8 thick slices white bread
1 litre milk

6 eggs
1 cup vanilla sugar
½ cup sultanas or raisins

Whisky sauce

1 cup sugar
2 tblsp water
100 grams butter

2 eggs
¼ cup whisky
¼ cup cream (optional)

Bread and butter pudding with whisky sauce

Serves 8-10

1. Spread four slices of the bread with the butter and make into sandwiches with the remaining four slices.
2. Place the bread into a large bowl and pour over the milk and set aside.
3. Beat the eggs and vanilla sugar together until the mixture is quite thick and creamy. Pour over the soaked bread with the sultanas or raisins and stir well.
4. Pour mixture into a well greased 6–8 cup capacity baking dish.
5. Bake in a water bath at 180°C for 1 hour or until a knife inserted comes out clean.
6. Serve warm with whisky sauce.

Whisky sauce

Put the sugar, water and butter into a small saucepan and heat gently, stirring constantly until the sugar has dissolved. Transfer the syrup to the top of a double saucepan and stir in the eggs and whisky. Cook over gently simmering water until the sauce has thickened. Stir in the cream if using. Makes ¾ cup.

Use a light wholemeal bread if you like. Do not use a heavy one as it will detract from the delicate flavour of the dish. You could also try brioche — very decadent then, but ever so wonderful

Cook's Tip:

Vanilla sugar can be easily made by placing a vanilla pod in a canister of sugar. I do this with all my caster sugar. However if you do not have it, add 1 teaspoon vanilla essence.

Hot ginger soufflé

Serves 4-6

This ginger soufflé is from Ann Boardman. If you have never made a soufflé before and are daunted by them, don't be. They can be prepared quite some way in advance and finished off just prior to eating. There are variations at the end for you too! Baked soufflés are fragile. The hot air trapped in the soufflé begins to escape once removed from the oven, causing the soufflé to collapse. Time it so that it will be served when you take it out of the oven.

1-2 tsp melted butter (for greasing the dish)
2 tblsp caster sugar (for coating the dish)
3 tblsp butter
3 tblsp flour
1 cup milk
4 eggs
1 egg white

2 tblsp finely chopped crystallized ginger
1 tsp finely grated orange rind
¾ tsp ground ginger
½ tsp ground cardamon
1 tblsp dark rum
3 tblsp caster sugar

1. First prepare the soufflé dish. Cut a double thickness of greaseproof paper to make a collar to fit around a 7-cup capacity soufflé dish. The collar must be 10 cm above the rim of the dish. Tie securely with string. Brush the inside of the dish and collar with melted butter. Sprinkle the first measure of caster sugar around the insides and collar until finely coated. Discard any excess.

2. Melt the butter in a saucepan. Add the flour and cook over a moderate heat for about 1 minute until frothy and the mixture is bubbling. Stir constantly and do not overcook as the butter will burn. Remove from the heat and stir in the milk, adding it a little at a time until all the milk has been added. Return to the heat and cook, stirring continuously until the mixture is smooth and thick. Allow to cool slightly.

3. Separate eggs. Place the 5 egg whites into a large scrupulously clean bowl.

4. Beat the egg yolks together. Do not over beat them, just until well blended. Add the warmed sauce to the egg yolks, mixing well. Stir in the crystallized ginger, orange rind, ginger, cardamon and rum, and mix well to combine.

5. Beat the egg whites until they are stiff. To see if they have been beaten until stiff, lift the beater from the egg whites and watch what form the egg whites take. If the peak of the egg white falls over gently, then it has reached the soft peak stage. Continue to beat until the egg-white peak just stands up. Do not beat the egg whites until they look dry. They should still have a sheen on them.

6. Sprinkle over the second measure of sugar and beat until the sugar is absorbed and the egg whites are glossy.

7. Mix 1 large spoonful of egg white into the sauce to lighten its texture. Using a large holed metal spoon, carefully cut and fold the egg whites into the sauce until the egg whites are just incorporated. There may still be a few streaks of egg white remaining. This will be okay. Do not overmix as you will begin to knock out the air that you have taken so much care to beat into the egg whites.

8. Pour the soufflé mixture into the prepared dish. The mixture should come about ¾ of the way up the dish.
9. Cook at 190°C for 30 minutes or until well risen and golden brown. Do not open the oven door to peep while cooking or the soufflé will collapse.
10. Cut the string, remove the paper collar and serve immediately.

Cook's Tip:

You can prepare the soufflé to step 8 and set aside until you are ready to cook and eat. If you do this, you will need to just gently warm the sauce before adding the egg whites. If you do not warm the sauce, then the egg whites will not fold in so easily and the soufflé will take a little longer to cook. When you reheat the sauce, do not bring it to the boil, only warm it.

Apple fruit crumble flan

Serves 6

Jazz up the apple crumble with a pastry base. Great with yoghurt or custard, this is a nice variation on an old family favourite.

1 cup wholemeal flour	*¼ cup milk*
½ cup flour	*¼ cup oats*
¼ cup brown sugar	*2 cups stewed apple*
100 grams butter	*½-1 cup berry fruit or sultanas*
1 tsp baking powder	

1. Put the flours and brown sugar into a food processor and pulse in the butter until it resembles crumbs. Remove ¾ cup of the crumb mixture and set aside.
2. Pulse the baking powder into the remaining mixture and mix in well. Pulse in sufficient milk to form a soft dough.
3. Turn onto a board, knead lightly and roll out to fit the base and sides of well greased 20 cm flan dish.
4. Bake blind at 200°C for 10 minutes. Remove the baking blind material and return to the oven for a further 5 minutes.★
5. Add the oats to the reserved ¾ cup crumb mixture and mix topping well.
6. Turn the apple and berry fruits or sultanas into the flan. Sprinkle over the topping.
7. Bake at 180°C for 20-25 minutes until hot and golden.

★See the introduction for the baking blind technique.

Creamy plum tart

Serves 6-8

Rather rich but delicious, this plum tart makes a special finish to a meal with friends.

1¼ cups flour
1 tsp baking powder
2 tblsp sugar

100 grams butter
3–4 tblsp milk

Filling

250-gram tub sour cream or light sour cream
2 eggs
2 tblsp caster sugar

½ tsp vanilla essence
6–8 plums, halved and stoned
ground cinnamon or allspice

1. Put the flour, baking powder and sugar into a food processor and pulse to sift.
2. Add the butter and mix until it resembles coarse crumbs. Pulse in sufficient milk to form a dough.
3. Turn onto a board and knead lightly. Wrap and chill for 30 minutes. Roll the pastry out to line the base and sides of a 20 cm flan dish. Bake blind for 12 minutes.★
4. Beat the sour cream, eggs, sugar and vanilla together. Pour into the pastry lined flan.
5. Arrange the plums cut-side up in the filling. Sprinkle with cinnamon.
6. Bake at 180°C for 50 minutes.
7. Dust with icing sugar before serving.

*See the introduction for the baking blind technique.

Cook's Tip:

A 400-gram can of fruit halves, well drained, can be substituted for fresh fruit. Apricots and plums are best.

Microwave fruity fudge pudding

Serves 4-6

Dessert in 10 minutes! This recipe is ideal for children to make. If you do not have a microwave, cook at 180°C for 40-50 minutes.

1 cup flour
2 tsp baking powder
¼ cup caster sugar
50 grams butter
½ cup milk

¼ cup dried fruit (optional)
1 tblsp cocoa
¾ cup brown sugar
1 cup boiling hot water

1. Sift the flour, baking powder and caster sugar together.
2. Rub in the butter. Stir in the milk and dried fruit.
3. Turn into a greased 6-cup capacity microwave-proof dish.
4. Sift the cocoa and brown sugar on top and pour over the boiling water.
5. Microwave on full power (100%) for 7 minutes. Stand 2 minutes before serving.
6. Serve with yoghurt or whipped cream.

My mum used to make this often when we were young. For a change, substitute oranges or mandarins for variety.

50 grams butter	¼ cup self rising flour
¾ cup caster sugar	1 cup milk
1 tblsp grated lemon rind	¼ cup lemon juice
3 eggs, separated	¼ tsp cream of tartar (optional)

1. Put the butter, sugar, lemon rind and egg yolks into a food processor and process until light, about 2 minutes.
2. Pulse in the flour, milk and lemon juice.
3. Put the egg whites in a clean bowl with the cream of tartar. Beat until they form stiff peaks but are not dry.
4. Fold the 2 mixtures together and pour into a well-greased 4-cup capacity oven-proof dish.
5. Bake at 160°C for 50-60 minutes in a bain marie.
6. The pudding will separate into a spongy cake on top and a thick tangy lemon sauce on the bottom. Serve with lashings of whipped cream.

Lemon delicious pudding

Serves 4-6

It looks like it won't work! The mixture is very sloppy. But it does and is delicious

Rich, thin, round shortbread layered between fruit and whipped cream make a simple but delightful dessert any time of the year, though summer is ideal.

3 cups flour	beaten egg or milk to glaze
1 cup caster sugar	about ¼ cup extra caster sugar
350 grams soft butter	fresh fruit
1 egg	sweetened whipped cream

1. Put the flour, sugar, butter and egg into a food processor.
2. Process until the dough forms a ball. Wrap in plastic wrap and refrigerate 1 hour.
3. Roll out on a floured board to 3 mm thickness and cut out 18-24 rounds.
4. Place on a greased tray and brush with beaten egg or milk to glaze. Sprinkle 6 sables with extra caster sugar.
5. Bake at 210°C for 15 minutes until golden.
6. Cool and keep in an airtight container.
7. To assemble, allow 3 sables per person. Prepare fruit and whip cream, sweeten with sugar and flavour with fruit liqueur if wished. Arrange fruit and a little cream on one sable, top with another sable and repeat the fruit and cream. Top with the sugared sable.

Summer sables

Serves 6–8 depending on size of sables

Golden syrup dumplings

Serves 4

1 cup self rising flour
2 tblsp butter

1 egg
¼ cup milk

Sauce

1 cup water
2 tblsp golden syrup

1 tblsp butter
3 tblsp brown sugar

1. Place the flour in a bowl and rub in the butter.
2. Make a well in the centre and add egg and milk. Mix with a knife.
3. Put the water, golden syrup, butter and brown sugar in a medium-sized saucepan. Bring to the boil.
4. Roll the dough into 6–8 oven-sized balls and place in the saucepan.
5. Cover and simmer for 15 minutes.
6. Serve hot with cream or yoghurt.

Upside-down pear tart with chocolate pastry

Serves 4–6

This is a variation on a tarte tartin, a traditional French dessert with the pastry cooked on top but served underneath. It's not complicated, but it is truly delicious, especially served with fruit yoghurt, cream or ice cream. In winter, I make this often when I'm entertaining.

1 cup flour
¼ cup cocoa
2 tblsp sugar
175 grams unsalted butter
2-4 tblsp cold water

5-6 very firm pears
50 grams butter
¼ cup sugar (brown, white or caster)
grated rind of 1 lemon or orange

1. Put the flour, cocoa, sugar and butter in a food processor and process until mixture resembles coarse crumbs.
2. Pulse in just enough water to bring the pastry to smallish moist balls of dough. (If you let the dough become a large ball in the processor it will become tough. It is best to stop processing before this happens.) Knead lightly and refrigerate.
3. Peel and core the pears.
4. Melt the butter, sugar and lemon or orange rind in a deep oven-proof frying pan. I suggest the pan be no wider than 27 cm.
5. Arrange the pear halves core side down, making sure they are close together. Place one half in the centre.
6. Cook on top of the stove for about 5 minutes or until a caramel sauce is formed.
7. Roll the pastry out to the diameter of the top of the frying pan. Lay the pastry over the top of the pears, tucking the edges around the inside of the pears in the pan.
8. Bake at 200°C for 20-25 minutes or until the pastry is crisp.
9. Stand for 5 minutes before turning upside down on a large plate to serve. Serve warm with remaining pan juices poured on top.

Variations:

- Use apples instead of pears. Or change spices to vary the flavour. My favourites include cardamom and ginger.
- If you do not have time to make the pastry, use a 400-gram packet frozen short pastry.
- Roll ground hazelnuts into the pastry — about ½ cup.
- Make a plain short pastry by using 1¼ cups flour and omitting the cocoa.

Passionfruit soufflé

Serves 4-6

I once ate at a fabulous restaurant in Melbourne called Brown's and was served a wonderful passionfruit soufflé. I've never been able to recreate it exactly, but this is my version. The method is a little different to the Ginger Soufflé also described in this chapter.

6 tblsp flour	4 egg yolks
50 grams butter	pulp of 4 passionfruit
1 cup milk	½ tsp cream of tartar
½ tsp vanilla essence or 1 vanilla pod	6 tblsp caster sugar
5 egg whites	

1. Prepare a 1½ litre soufflé dish first. Grease the base and sides thoroughly and dust with caster sugar.
2. Mix the flour and butter to a smooth paste.
3. Bring the milk, vanilla essence or vanilla pod to the boil. If using a vanilla pod, scrape out some of the seeds and remove the pod.
4. Using a whisk, vigorously stir the butter and flour mixture into the milk and cook until the custard is thick. Remove from the heat and add one of the egg whites, beating well.
5. Add the egg yolks and passionfruit and mix thoroughly.
6. In a clean bowl, beat the remaining egg whites with the cream of tartar until stiff but not dry. Gradually beat in the sugar until you obtain a soft meringue consistency.
7. Stir one-third of the meringue mixture into the passionfruit custard. Then carefully fold the remaining meringue mixture in. Turn into the prepared soufflé dish.
8. Bake at 200°C for 30-35 minutes.
9. Serve with fruit if wished.

Cook's Tip:

To test if a soufflé is cooked, carefully shake the dish in the oven. If the soufflé 'wobbles' violently, it is not cooked. If it 'wobbles' a little in the centre then it is ready. The centre of a soufflé should never be dry. It should still have a little bit of wet mixture to serve as a sauce.

Variations:

- Omit the passionfruit and add an extra teaspoon of vanilla essence.
- Add 1 tablespoon grated lemon or orange rind in place of the passionfruit.

Summer coconut slice

Serves 6–8

Use summer's berry bounty to vary this slice. Poached and sliced apricots or peaches are also wonderful in place of berry fruits.

100 grams butter	*1 cup flour*
½ cup caster sugar	*½ tsp baking soda*
2 eggs	*½ cup coconut*
1 tsp vanilla essence	*½ cup sour cream (150-gram tub)*

Syrup
2 tblsp caster sugar
¼ cup water

Fruit
1 punnet strawberries or 2 punnets boysenberries or raspberries
about ¼ cup jam (flavour to match the choice of berries)

1. Beat the butter, caster sugar, eggs and vanilla essence in a food processor until creamy.
2. Sift the flour and baking soda together. Pulse into the creamed mixture with the coconut and sour cream.
3. Spread the mixture into a greased, floured and lined 28 cm × 20 cm sponge roll tin. Bake at 180°C for 15-20 minutes until cooked. Leave in the tin.
4. Make the syrup by boiling the sugar and water together for 1 minute until the sugar has dissolved.
6. When the cake is cooked, carefully drizzle over half the syrup. When cold, turn the cake onto a serving plate.
7. Decorate with the berries. Mix the ¼ cup of jam with the remaining syrup. Carefully decorate the berries with the jam. Serve with whipped cream or yoghurt.

Peach and almond crumble

Serves 6–8

Crumbles can be varied so much. I have added rolled oats to this one.

½ cup water	*¼ cup rolled oats*
3 tblsp honey	*¼ cup coconut*
4 large peaches	*2 tblsp brown sugar*
½ cup flour	*2 tblsp sliced almonds*
50 grams butter	

1. Place water and honey in a small saucepan. Heat till simmering. Add peaches, cover and simmer gently for about 10 minutes or until peaches are soft. Cool. Peel peaches and slice.
2. Place sliced peaches in shallow baking dish and pour over the syrup they were cooked in.

3. Put the flour and butter into a food processor and process until the mixture resembles crumbs.

4. Pulse in the rolled oats, coconut, brown sugar and almonds.

5. Sprinkle mixture over peaches. Bake at 180°C for 15 minutes or until light golden brown.

Variations:

- In place of fresh peaches you may like to use canned sliced peaches. Omit water and honey and use half the syrup from the can.
- Try using other stone fruit such as plums, apricots or nectarines.
- Try using other nuts in place of almonds, such as walnuts.

Baked lemon and ricotta cheesecake

Serves 6-8

Do not think of cheesecakes as 1970s gelatin-and-condensed-milk only. Baked cheesecakes are a world away. I've made this one with a phyllo pastry base and a ricotta cheese filling.

1 cup ricotta cheese
1 cup light sour cream
3 eggs
¼ cup sugar
1 tsp grated lemon rind

2 tblsp lemon juice
½ cup sultanas
25 grams melted butter
4 sheets phyllo pastry

You can make this with quark or a richer version using cream cheese.

1. Place ricotta cheese, sour cream, eggs, sugar, lemon rind and lemon juice in a food processor and process until well combined. Pulse in sultanas.

2. Brush a 20 cm square baking dish with butter.

3. Cut the phyllo pastry sheets in half, to give 8 sheets. Brush the first sheet lightly with butter or margarine and place a second sheet of phyllo on top. Arrange in the dish. Continue until all sheets are layered together.

4. Pour in the cheese mixture.

5. Bake at 180°C for 30-40 minutes or until the filling is just firm to touch.

6. When cold, cut and serve sprinkled with icing sugar.

Variations:

- In place of sultanas, use other dried fruit such as raisins, currants or chopped dried apricots.
- Use orange rind and juice in place of lemon.

Cook's Tip:

If you do not have a food processor you can mix all the ingredients together in a bowl.

Pecan meringue crepes

Serves 8

I made this recipe for a wonderful class on Creole and Cajun cuisine at Auckland's Epicurean Workshop. It is a super dessert: lightly cooked meringue wrapped in a spicy crepe and filled with a pecan sauce — truly yumptious!

½ cup flour	1 tblsp sugar
pinch salt	1 egg
⅛ tsp grated nutmeg	1 cup milk

Filling

1 cup pecan nuts	½ cup double cream
½ cup corn syrup	3 egg whites
1 egg yolk	½ cup icing sugar
3 tblsp cooled melted butter	1–2 tblsp rum
½ tsp vanilla essence	

1. Sift the flour, salt, nutmeg and sugar into a bowl and make a well in the centre.
2. Beat the egg and milk together. Pour the liquid gradually into the flour, stirring to incorporate. Mix well. Strain through a sieve and set aside for 30 minutes.
3. Lightly grease a pancake pan and heat.
4. Pick up the pan and pour in about 2 tablespoons of batter, quickly tilting the pan so the batter coats the bottom and sides.
5. Cook only on one side until the edges curl and the bottom is golden brown. Turn out crepe and repeat with remaining batter. Cover crepes with a damp cloth (they can be prepared in advance and frozen if wished).
6. Place the pecans in a 200°C oven for 5-8 minutes until dark in colour. Allow to cool and chop finely.
7. In a bowl mix together the corn syrup, egg yolk, melted butter, vanilla essence and pecans. Stir in the double cream. Set sauce aside.
8. In a clean bowl beat the egg whites until frothy. Add the icing sugar and continue beating until they form stiff peaks. Fold in the rum.
9. Fold ½ a cup of the meringue into the reserved pecan sauce.
10. Place one crepe, brown side down, on a dinner plate. Spoon 2 tablespoonfuls of pecan sauce down the middle. Cover the sauce with large dollops of meringue (the meringue needs to be divided roughly into eighths). Roll crepe into thirds, then turn it over so it is seam-side down on the plate. Repeat with remaining crepes and filling.
11. Bake the crepes at 220°C for about 5-7 minutes, until the meringue puffs up.
12. Remove from the oven and serve immediately with any remaining pecan sauce.

Browning the butter before brushing it onto the phyllo gives a warm nutty flavour to this fresh-tasting strudel.

100 grams butter
4 cooking apples
2 fresh mangoes or 400-gram can, well drained

2 tblsp sugar
2 tblsp lemon juice
10–12 sheets phyllo pastry
70-gram pkt ground almonds

Custard

1 cup coconut cream
1 cup milk or cream
1 vanilla pod or ½ tsp pure vanilla essence

6 egg yolks
¼ cup sugar

Burnt mango and apple strudel with coconut and vanilla custard

Serves 6-8

1. Melt the butter in a saucepan. Continue to cook once the butter is melted until it has become a deep nut-brown colour but is not burnt. Remove from the heat and set aside on a damp cloth. This will stop the butter from browning any further.
2. Peel, core and very finely slice the apples. Cut the mango in two halves by slicing down each of the long sides by the central flat seed. Peel the skin away with a knife from each half and slice finely. Toss the apples, mangoes, sugar and lemon juice together.
3. Take one sheet of phyllo pastry and brush it with the melted butter. Place another sheet on top and brush with butter. Sprinkle over one tablespoon of the almonds. Place a third sheet on top, butter and then top with another sheet of phyllo, this time repeating the butter and almond process. Continue in this fashion until all the phyllo is used up.
4. Arrange the apple and mango slices lengthwise down the pastry. Fold over the short edges and roll up to completely secure the filling. Place the strudel on a greased tray, seam side down.
5. Brush liberally with the nut-brown butter.
6. Bake at 180°C for 40 minutes until the phyllo is golden and the apples are cooked.
7. Serve hot with coconut and vanilla custard.

Coconut and vanilla custard

Heat the coconut cream, milk and vanilla pod together until boiling point. Stand for 5 minutes. Put the egg yolks and sugar in the top of a double boiler and mix well. Gradually pour in the milk, stirring constantly. Cook the custard over simmering water, stirring all the time, until the custard has thickened. Cool. (Remove the vanilla pod and wash in warm water. Dry and store for re-use.)

Cook's Tip:

While pure vanilla essence is more expensive to buy, it is well worth the difference. Imitation vanilla has a harsh taste. You can make your own supply and have it on hand in bulk. Take one vanilla pod and split it open. Place it in a jar and cover it with ¾ cup vodka. Store tightly sealed for 4-6 months. Use as required.

Apple almond tart

Serves 4-6

1¼ cups pure flour
pinch salt
100 grams butter

1 egg yolk
1 tblsp ice cold water

Almond cream
100 grams unsalted butter
½ cup caster sugar
1 egg
1 egg yolk

¼ cup pure flour
1 cup ground almonds
1 tblsp cream

Filling
5 small ripe eating apples
¼-½ cup smooth apricot jam
1 tblsp lemon juice

1. Sift the flour and the salt. Rub in the butter.
2. Mix together the egg yolk and the water.
3. Make a well in the centre of the flour mixture and add the egg. Mix gently to a firm dough. Wrap in paper and chill for 30 minutes.
4. Use the pastry to line a 25 cm flan ring. Prick the bottom lightly with a fork.
5. Spread the almond cream into the pastry case.
6. Peel the apples. Halve and core them, retaining their shape. Slice the half-apples, keeping all the slices together in their original order.
7. Arrange the apples, in the almond cream, around the side of the dish, rounded side up, so that the slices overlap slightly. Place an apple half in the middle and press firmly into the cream.
8. Melt the jam slowly with the lemon juice. Spoon half of it over the apples.
9. Bake for 15 minutes at 220°C, then a further 20 minutes at 180°C. Remove from the oven when the pastry is crisp, the apples are cooked and the almond cream is risen and brown. If the mixture begins to brown too quickly, lower temperature by 20°C. Brush the flat top with the remaining jam mixture and return to the oven for a further 10 minutes. Serve warm.

Almond cream
Beat the butter until it is soft. Add the sugar and continue to beat until pale and creamy. Add the egg, egg yolk, flour, almonds and cream.

This cake improves on keeping and should be served with fresh fruits and whipped cream for an elegant dessert.

Gateau Breton

Serves 4–6

250 grams flour
pinch salt
250 grams sugar
250 grams unsalted butter, at room temperature
6 egg yolks (reserve 1 teaspoon of yolk for glaze)

1. Sift flour and salt onto marble board or kitchen bench. Make a large well in the centre. Put sugar, butter and egg yolks in well. Work with fingertips until the mixture is smooth, then gradually work in the flour using fingers and heel of hand in a rocking motion — it will be thick and sticky.
2. Flatten dough to fit a well greased 23 cm flan tin, smoothing top with a wet hand.
3. Brush surface with reserved egg yolk. Use a fork to mark a lattice pattern on top. Rest in fridge 10 minutes.
4. Place in a 190°C oven. Immediately turn to 170°C, and bake 30 minutes, or until cake is golden and has shrunk from the sides of the tin. Leave to cool 10 minutes, then turn out onto a wire rack.

Walnut and lemon tart

Serves 8-10

175 grams butter
1 cup icing sugar
1 egg

1 egg yolk (left over from filling)
2½ cups flour

Filling

2 cups walnuts
½ cup caster sugar
¼ cup icing sugar

2 egg whites (reserve 1 egg yolk to glaze)
grated rind 1 lemon

1. Put the butter, icing sugar, egg and egg yolk in a food processor. Process until the mixture is well blended.
2. Add flour and pulse to mix together.
3. Press half the dough into the greased base and sides of a 22-24 cm loose-bottom flan tin.
4. Finely chop the walnuts. Mix together with the caster sugar, icing sugar, egg whites and lemon rind. Beat well. Pour into the flan and spread out evenly.
5. Roll out the remaining pastry to cover the top. Press the edges together. Brush with beaten egg or milk to glaze and sprinkle with extra caster sugar if wished.
6. Place a baking tray in a 200°C oven for 10 minutes before placing the tart on top. Bake for 10 minutes, then reduce heat to 170°C for a further 30 minutes.
7. Serve hot or cold.

ICINGS
AND
FILLINGS

Decorating the top of biscuits and slices with icings or decorating and filling cakes with a simple icing or filling can enhance the taste and appearance of your baking. The following are the basic icings that I use regularly.

Butter icing

This can be used as an icing or as a filling.

100 grams butter
1½ cups icing sugar
few drops vanilla essence
about 1-2 tblsp milk

1. Beat the butter until it is pale and fluffy.
2. Sift the icing sugar and beat into the creamed butter with the vanilla essence and sufficient milk until you have a fluffy light mixture. If you need the mixture to spread more easily, then add a little more milk.

Variations:
- Lemon — add the grated rind of 1 lemon and use lemon juice in place of the milk.
- Orange — add the grated rind of 1 orange and use orange juice in place of the milk.
- Chocolate — heat the 2 tablespoons of milk and dissolve 2 tablespoons cocoa. Allow to cool. Add to the creamed butter and icing sugar mixture.

Cook's Tip:

Because of its thick spreadable nature, you can make butter icing into swirls or patterns with a knife. It can be easily piped into decorative patterns on top or around the edges of a cake.

Opposite: Outrageous Pecan Toffee Pud (page 169).
Following page: Golden Syrup Dumplings (page 176).

- Coffee — heat the 2 tablespoons of milk and dissolve 1 tablespoon coffee. Allow to cool before adding to the icing.
- Almond — add 1 drop of almond essence to the mixture and about ½ cup finely chopped toasted almonds.
- Mocha — dissolve 1 tablespoon cocoa and 1 teaspoon coffee in the 2 tablespoons of (hot) milk and allow to cool before adding to the icing.

Cream cheese icing

This is not a particularly sweet version.

250-gram tub cream cheese
¼ cup icing sugar
grated rind ½ lemon

1. Beat the cream cheese and icing sugar together until the icing sugar has dissolved and the mixture is light and creamy.
2. Beat in the lemon rind.

Variation:
Use 2 tablespoons honey in place of the icing sugar.

Coffee fudge icing

50 grams butter
¾ cup brown sugar
2 tblsp coffee
2 tblsp milk (not trim)
1½ cups icing sugar

1. In a saucepan put the butter, brown sugar, coffee and milk. Bring to the boil, stirring constantly. Simmer for about 3 minutes stirring frequently.
2. Remove from the heat and beat in the sifted icing sugar. Beat until thick and smooth, about 2 minutes. Use while warm.

Variation:
Chocolate — use 100 grams cooking chocolate in place of the coffee.

Preceding page: Summer Coconut Slice (page 178).
Opposite: Honey-scented White Bread in various shapes (page 131), with Bagels (page 134).

Glacé icing

This is quicker to make than Butter Icing and is not as rich.

1½ cups icing sugar
1 tsp melted butter (optional)
2-3 tblsp warm water or milk

1. Sift the icing sugar into a bowl.
2. Add the melted butter and sufficient warm water or milk to make a smooth thick icing that can spread easily.

Variations:
*   Passionfruit — add the grated rind of half a lemon and the strained pulp of a passionfruit to the icing. Add water if necessary. You can add the pips from the passionfruit if wished.
*   Lemon or orange — use the grated rind of 1 lemon or orange and its juice to make the icing in place of the milk or water.
*   Chocolate — dissolve 1 tablespoon cocoa in the hot milk or water and allow to cool. Mix in the sifted icing sugar and sufficient extra milk or water to reach the desired consistency.
*   Ginger — add 1 teaspoon ground ginger to the icing sugar before sifting.
*   Spice — add ½ teaspoon of mixed spice to the icing sugar before sifting. Use one favourite spice or a combination.
*   Mocha — dissolve 1 teaspoon coffee and 1 teaspoon cocoa in hot water before mixing with the remaining icing ingredients.
*   Liqueur — use your favourite liqueur in place of the water.
*   Orange blossom — add 1 or 2 drops of orange blossom water to the icing.
*   Rosewater — add 1 or 2 drops of rosewater to the icing. Use to decorate the top of a cake with fresh rose petals.

How to Use
Glacé icing can be used to coat the top and sides of a cake. Place the cake on a cake rack. Pour the icing over the cake, making sure that you pour it into the centre. The icing will then run evenly down the sides of the cake. You need to use a knife to help guide it around the sides, filling up any gaps. If there is any icing on the tray beneath, it can be gathered up and re-used, so long as there are no cake crumbs in the mixture.

Feathering is easy to do and looks great, but you will require a second quantity of another colour. Coat the cake with the larger quantity of icing. Working quickly before this has had time to set, fill an icing bag fitted with a narrow nozzle with the second quantity of icing. Pipe parallel lines about 1-2 cm apart on top of the cake. Quickly draw the point of a skewer across the lines first in one direction and then in the other, spacing them the same widths apart as the lines of icing. Allow to set.

Spider's webs follow the same principle as feathering. Cover the cake with the first quantity of icing. Pipe concentric circles about 1-1.5 cm apart on top with the second quantity of icing. Starting at the centre, quickly draw the point of a skewer outwards to the edge of the cake. Continue this, spacing the strokes evenly and doing them only in one direction. This makes an ideal decoration for the top of a Halloween party cake.

Acknowledgements

Friends are a most priceless gift and without the help of so many of them over the past year I am sure this book would never have been finished. Like any project, enthusiasm runs high at the beginning. As the project proceeds, it is the support of those who share the dream that make another long night in the kitchen seem not so bad and even rewarding when they enjoy the results over a cup of tea. To the baking taste-testers, who every Sunday night would swap a drink for a load of baking, thank you for the endless eating — yes, someone had to do it! Lynne and Greg, Debbie and Drew, Kevin, Liz and Cam, Roya and Carl, Simon and Anna. I think we were all somewhat relieved when the more than 200 recipes were finally tested!! My Sunday nights are not the same without the weekly baking drop-offs.

Thanks to Richard, for his advice, and his wife Elise.

Thanks to my best friends, Louise and Adrienne, for their encouragement when the nights got long behind the wordprocessor and to Alan Gillard, my friend and photographer for some 10 years now, for the wonderful photographs in this book. All four of us shared so many wonderful laughs as we worked together each weekend.

When the work overloaded, I was especially lucky to have the support of two very competent food consultants Ann Boardman and Pauline Willoughby, who were always there and who helped relieve the stress levels.

I am fortunate to have had the company of a fun flatmate, Eric, who put up with the midnight cooking. And then there is Sue, who helped type the book up, and Jane from Trumps and Jocelyn from The Studio who loaned props for my photographs. I have worked with some great people on this book: Dennis Housby, who did the fabulously creative drawings, and Ann Clifford, my editor from Wellington, who began this dream with a simple phone call and whose advice and knowledge I respect.

And there are very special thank yous to Barbara Dilger in Tasmania for her recipes, and to Phyl, a special aunt in Tauranga, for her thoughtful and inspiring advice about this book and my Next column. When the ideas get too carried away I know that they, and I, will be brought down-to-earth. Thanks also to Tui Flower, who guided me in the profession of food writing, and Joan, my favourite sister-in-law, and all her family for so openly sharing their collection of recipes, which are included in this book.

Thanks to Warwick for his time, help, patience and love in getting this book to the publishers on time. Without him, so much around my home and this book would never have been completed.

And the final special thank you to my Mum, Dad and brother Adrian, who sent encouraging and supportive letters from across the sea each week, as they have done for 11 years, as they realised that to test and develop each of these recipes was no small task. They are the best.

To everyone, thank you.

Allyson

INDEX

INDEX OF COOK'S TIPS